A COLLECTION OF WRITINGS TO AWAKEN YOUR MIND
TO POSITIVE THINKING, AN ATTITUDE OF GRATITUDE,
AND SPIRITUAL AWARENESS

celubrious

A CELEBRATION OF LIFE

SECOND EDITION

DENNIS A. MARTIN

TATE PUBLISHING
AND ENTERPRISES, LLC

Celubrious Messages: A Celebration of Life
Copyright © 2013 by Dennis A. Martin. All rights reserved.

This title is also available as a Tate Out Loud product. Visit www.tatepublishing.com for more information.

Also visit www.celubrious.net for more information.

No part of this publication may be reproduced, stored in a retrieval system or transmitted in any way by any means, electronic, mechanical, photocopy, recording or otherwise without the prior permission of the author except as provided by USA copyright law.

All Scriptures are taken from the *Holy Bible, New International Version* ®, Copyright © 1973, 1978, 1984 by International Bible Society. Used by permission of Zondervan Publishing House. All rights reserved.

The opinions expressed by the author are not necessarily those of Tate Publishing, LLC.

Published by Tate Publishing & Enterprises, LLC
127 E. Trade Center Terrace | Mustang, Oklahoma 73064 USA
1.888.361.9473 | www.tatepublishing.com

Tate Publishing is committed to excellence in the publishing industry. The company reflects the philosophy established by the founders, based on Psalm 68:11,
"The Lord gave the word and great was the company of those who published it."

Book design copyright © 2013 by Tate Publishing, LLC. All rights reserved.
Cover design by Lynly D. Taylor
Interior design by Jacob Crissup

Published in the United States of America

ISBN: 978-1-62902-464-6
Religion / Christian Life / Inspirational
Self-Help / Personal Growth
13.08.05

Introduction

2nd Edition of "Celubrious" a celebration of life

THIS is the beginning of a new day; another gift and blessing from your maker. God has given you this whole day to use as you will in the best possible way. He allows you choice and you can choose to waste the day or use it for good. But remember; what you choose to do today is important, because you are exchanging a day of your life for it. When tomorrow comes, this day will be gone forever, leaving something you have traded for it. You should want this day to be for gain, not loss; good, not evil; success, not failure; all this in order that you shall not regret the price you have paid for it. Guess what? If you choose correctly with your trust in Him and with love and enthusiasm, this day may just be the day all of your dreams come true.

An acquaintance of mine sadly told me that pondering back on his youth he was dying to finish high school, and start college. And then he was dying to finish college, and start working. Then he was dying to marry and have children. And then he was dying to have them grow older so he could go back to work. But then he was dying to retire, and now he's dying. All of a sudden, he realized he forgot to live! I hope this does not reflect your life and that you appreciate you current situation and enjoy each and every day.

I recently received this story from a dear friend and I would like to share it. It seems appropriate for those of us who celebrate life's daily journey with all of its heartbreaking experiences as well as its joyous and happy experiences.

"And Then It's Winter"

You know...Time has a way of moving quickly and catching us unaware of the passing years. It seems like just yesterday that we were young, just married and embarking on a new life with a soul-mate. Yet in a way, it seems like eons ago, and we wonder where all the years went. We know that we lived them all and occasionally have glimpses of how it was back then. Yet the winter of our life's catches us by surprise...How did we get here so fast? Where did the years go and where did our youth go? We remember seeing older people through the years and thinking that being like those older people was years away from us and so far off that we could not fathom it or imagine fully what it would be like.

Our friends are retired and getting gray, some are in better and some worse shape; not like the ones that we remember when they were young and vibrant. Like us, their age is beginning to show and we are now those older folks that we used to see and never thought we'd be. We enter into this new season of our life unprepared for all the aches and pains and the loss of strength and ability to do things that we wished we had done but never did. Yes, there may be regrets about things we wished we had or hadn't done. But indeed, there are many things we have enjoyed doing or in some cases glad we didn't do during our lifetime. If you're not in your winter yet...let me remind you, that it will be here faster than you think. So, whatever you would like to accomplish in your life please do it quickly! Don't put things off too long!! Life goes by quickly. Do what you can today, as you can never be sure you will see all the seasons that you would like to see. Live for today and say all the things that you want your loved ones to remember you saying and hope that they appreciate and love you for all the things that you have done for them. "Life" is God's gift to you. The way you live your life is your gift to those who come after you. Make each and every day a fantastic one!

As you enjoy and reflect on the readings and thoughts from this second edition of "Celubrious" my wish for you is to celebrate your life; Live it well! Enjoy it! Do something for fun! Be happy! And above all be thank-full for your blessings! And when you have read and digested the messages I hope you can say WOW! What a wonderful day this is to have learned that maybe God's purpose for me in life is to give birth to myself and to become all that my potential will allow me to become. In your celebration; hopefully you will be able to reminisce on life with delight, joy and ecstasy in your heart. It's too bad we didn't learn sooner "To know that you do not know is the best."

Dedication

This book is dedicated to my three number-one critics and initial editors of the morning messages when working was a part of my life: George Bakke, Valerie Jernigan, and Bob Amick. Each of them claims that I don't know how to use the spell check or the grammar check on my computer. George would grade the morning messages and give me a smiley face when the message was a "go" and a sad face for a "no go," when there were a few grammatical or spelling errors and needed correction. George has gone on to be with his Lord and Savior now, but I know he still grades my work and smiles down instead of sending happy faces when I do well. To all three of my friends, you have my eternal gratitude.

This 2nd edition of "Celubrious" is dedicated to my families the Martins and Murphys for their support, understanding, and appreciation of love we all share.

My Sincere Appreciations

First and foremost, I want to thank my Lord and Savior for giving me the ability to put the "celubrious" material together. My appreciation can be summed up by this quote from Mother Teresa: "I don't claim anything of the work. It is His work. I am like a little pencil in His hand. That is all. He does the thinking. He does the writing. The pencil has nothing to do with it. The pencil has only been allowed to be used."

To all those people (you know who you are) who have encouraged me to put my "Morning Messages" into a book, I thank you from the bottom of my heart. I especially want to thank my wife and forever friend, Patricia Murphy-Martin. One of the hardest parts of writing is getting out of bed, sitting at the computer, and getting on with it. If you sit back and just look at how big the project is and how overwhelming it is, you'll never finish. She was the gal behind the guy, and she was most responsible for assuring that I stayed motivated. She alone kept this bunny rabbit energized. Patti, my daily editor, you get the thunder for the final product. Without you the book would not have been legible, let alone produced. Patti, George, Bob, and Valerie, if I could give you all one gift, I would give you the ability to see yourself as others see you so you would know how very special you are.

Foreword

Long before Mr. Martin's *Celubrious* hit the Internet, the daily inspirational was an interoffice e-mail publication named the "Morning Message." It was initially greeted with cynicism and sarcasm. The initial select members of the workforce who were lucky enough to receive the words of encouragement, as well as Valerie Jernigan and me, often referred to it as the "Mourning Message." Its most cynical critic (me) would send back responses that were (although tongue-in-cheek) somewhat negative about the publication. Who was this man who tried to perk up the workforce everyday? When I read it first thing in the morning, I was still half-asleep and dreading the day ahead of me. This changed over the months and years ahead and I became one of Mr. Martin's greatest fans. I often assisted him by editing and spell-checking his messages.

Mr. Martin's greatest critic was not me, however. It was George. George was an elderly gentleman who had incurable throat cancer but continued to work because he wanted to be around people. He was offered disability insurance but refused it, preferring instead to show up at the office at 7 a.m. to review the message before publication. George was not a computer or e-mail savvy person. Since he could not speak due to the advanced stage of his illness, after reviewing the daily message, George would simply pass Mr.

Martin a piece of paper with his constructive rating. The rating system consisted of smiley faces. That's right, smiley faces. A frown meant you struck out. One smiley: a single. Two smileys: good—a double. Three smileys: great—a triple. Four smileys: fantastic—a homerun.

George, I'm certain you're watching us from high above, reading *Celubrious* and critiquing the book. And I am certain you've given it a five-smiley, grand slam rating.

-Robert Blair Amick
Aerostat Site Manager
Lockheed Martin Systems Management (Retired)

Prologue

Who could have imagined that writing a book would have evolved from sharing some positive thoughts and attitudes with coworkers each morning via inter-office e-mail?

Now, the "celubrious" messages are being sent nationwide to hundreds of people on a daily basis and are forwarded by them to their families, friends, and coworkers. Many have told me they forward them around the country, some post them in their offices, and others take them home. Many have thanked me for the daily messages and, in some cases, have said their lives have been altered because of the messages. Wow! When that happens, the motivation factor for not quitting goes way up. When asked why I do the messages, my response is that these messages do more for me than anyone who receives them, and that Someone greater than me provides the daily inspiration to prepare them. Some people help spread love and positive thinking through different ministries, but I believe that mine is via the e-mail and through this book about celebrating life. Others have questioned how one man can be so positive and exceedingly happy. Their question is answered with this question: Do you know how awesome it is to have someone tell you that your e-mail of a "celubrious" message or a random reflection helped get them through the day? Or that somehow the message influenced them in their outlook on life? Or acknowledging the fact that their positive greetings, smiles, and thankfulness have become so infectious? In order to achieve that positive attitude and that level of happiness, always remember if a person is bitter, negative, and does not appear to be happy with life, they cannot help but become what they project. When you project an aura of happiness by thinking and speaking positively and you keep a thankful attitude with a smile, you also cannot help but become what you project.

We do not find the meaning of life alone, but only with another.
—*Dennis & Patti Martin*

Before and after love are you the same person? Before love you were a lamp that shed no light; when in love you became a lamp that was burning and shedding light. While in love you found the courage to risk and try again. You found new behaviors for old ways and ventured into places in your mind and heart you never explored before. Actually love reveals your "self" to you and allows you to discover the burning lamp in another. Love seems to have perfect vision and it makes it possible for you to see as you have never seen before. You may ask yourself "how can I be the same person after love?" You can move on to new love and be the better for it. Who knows - with new love you may be the best you can be.

Thoughts to Ponder

- Perfection is not a requirement to love, but honesty is.
- Remember the human spirit is stronger than anything that can happen to it.
- When you feel down because you didn't get what you want, just sit tight and be happy because God is thinking of something better to give you.
- "Love that asketh love again, finds the barter naught but pain. Love that giveth in full store, aye receives as much and more." (Dinah Mulock Craik)

"The best way to prepare for life is to begin to live."
—*Noel Watkins*

A good way to begin living is to appreciate your friends and shower your loved ones with love. I've said it before "Since you are a work in progress you need to keep working on your inner-self beginning with that positive attitude." So try to spend more time with family and friends, send that card or letter you've been putting off, give a little extra squeeze with the next hug and spend more time with your spouse. You will never succeed by wishes and desires alone because those with out the courage to act will only breed complacency. Begin living now by starting your own internal web site (Prepare your soul and act on it now.org) Visit those friends you say you want to see and plan that vacation even if you can't afford it. If you don't go, plan the next trip and the one after that but keep on trying until it happens. Maybe your internal web site should be (Prepare positive attitude. Net) with the motto of, "Procrastination is opportunity's assassin and that someday is not a day of the week." Don't procrastinate, it is shameful, weak and despicable to desire and want things and then not make every effort to get them. And remember all things are possible with a little effort on your part and help from above. Now is the time to get your search engine running with your own internal web site you might call (Prepare each day with prayer.com)

Thoughts to Ponder

- Tomorrow is the day when idlers work, and fools reform.
- Be a faithful friend because it is the medicine of life.
- Each day can be a triumph as long as you are engaged in life.
- Not recommended—"Never put off until tomorrow what you can do the day after tomorrow." Mark Twain.

"It's choice—not chance, that determines your destiny."
—Bob & Barbra Amick

In the theater of life; if fate meant for you to lose, you should give it a good fight anyhow. Your heart and soul is the control room in your theater of life. When everything seems to be out of control it's as if the film strip in your projector has gone off of the sprockets. Is your control room empty, is your projector broken? Guess what? In reality you are the projectionist, and you should be in control all the time with your Lord at you side. Tragic events happen to most of us in our life, but what's important is that you don't run away from them. You need to own up to them and to overcome them without bellyaching, complaining, showing a bad attitude of pessimism, because that pessimism can easily become a normal routine. Try being the optimistic. Be the one to make opportunities out of difficulties not difficulties out of opportunities. No matter how big you perceive the problem to be, take one little positive step towards the solution by trying something new. If it doesn't work try another approach and then try again. As long as you don't do the same thing twice you will eventually use up all the wrong ways. It's your choice, your destiny!

Thoughts to Ponder

- Since destiny is not a matter of chance but rather of choice it should not be waited for but should be achieved.
- To treat your problems with imagination is one thing, but to imagine you problems is another.
- Remember that a little reed, bending to the force of the wind, will soon stand upright again when the storm has passed over.
- Men are not prisoners of fate, but only prisoners of their own minds. "Franklin D. Roosevelt"

> *"Get over thinking that only the young have purpose in life. As long as you breath; you have a purpose, a reason and influence."*
>
> —*Tommy Murphy*

No matter how old you are when you begin to realize that you have purpose and meaning in your life; life itself, will be more enjoyable and be filled with much more happiness. So if you learn anything today, learn that your life has purpose, meaning and worth and the worth of your life comes not in what you do or by whom you know, but, with whom you are. Read, think and digest this! You are special and the effect you have on others is profound, and don't ever forget it. The Lord has a specific plan for YOU! You are not here merely to be a background character in someone else's movie. Even if you don't know what that plan is, your existence and the decisions you make affect all those around you and without your existence nothing would be the same. Every individual you have ever spoken to and every place you have ever been would not be the same without your existence. Keep this in mind and remind yourself, that if God's plan and mission for your life were finished, He would have already invited you to come home.

Thoughts to Ponder

- Life does not care about what you want—just about what you need
- If God made you then earth must have some purpose for you.
- Life is an irony in that hardly anyone gets out of it alive.
- "Don't bite the hand that feeds you." Well maybe you should, if it prevents you from a feeling of self worth or of being the real you.

> *"Aging seems to be the only available way to live a long life."*
>
> —*Louise & Jim Cooper*

I know it sounds weird but I feel younger now than I did at twenty. Have you ever heard, "The best tunes are played on the oldest fiddles?" Well the other evening I was enjoying music in the park by a group that had to be almost as old as me with instruments that were just as old and probably the originals their parents bought them. In this case the band had an accordion player and a stand up base fiddle and yes you guessed it the music was wonderful and enjoyed by all. When's the last time you heard an accordion? It's amazing how fast time flies and how your attitude can change over the years. It seemed like only yesterday when I thought that only older people would waste their time sitting in the park listening and dancing to oldies. Moods and emotions are ever changing. None will last forever. In my era it was dancing the jitter bug or the bop. Well guess who's eating those famous words now of, "You'll never catch me doing that." The only thing I can say is it's a sad age but it's nice to ripen. Here—here's to a long, long life!

Thoughts to Ponder

- You may delay but time will not.
- You will only be as miserable as you think you are.
- Things turn out best for the people who make the best out of the way things turn out.
- A man can't change the road he has covered—it's the path up ahead that counts.

"Change your thoughts and you change your world."
—*Bob Pennington*

I've heard it said, "Think you can, think you can't; either way, you'll be right." The way in which you think of yourself has everything to do with how you see the world and how the world sees you. Positive thinking is especially helpful for your mind-set and self image when your life seems cloudy and the storms of turmoil are inevitable. In life, pain and sorrow is inevitable but the length of your grief, anguish and ultimately your happiness is optional by changing your thoughts or with a little inner feelings adjustment. No matter the situation or the forecast you need to say to yourself, here is an opportunity for me to celebrate life like never before, to use my own power, to use my own ability and faith to overcome this adversity. Altering your thoughts and views in a positive way is never easy! So always remember; that changing your mind's inner attitude will always change the outer aspect of your life. And when it comes to the questioning of your life and attitude, remember with faith you are the answer to the problems of your life and your attitude. You can choose to be solution.

Thoughts to Ponder

- Every tomorrow has two handles. You can take hold of tomorrow with the handle of anxiety or the positive handle of faith.
- A positive way of thinking may not solve all your problems, but it will annoy enough people to make it worth the effort.
- There are three ingredients in the good life; learning, earning and yearning.
- In the last few years if you haven't thrown out some negative feelings and added a few positive ones—You must be dead!

"The best way to know God is to love many things"
—DeNise Martin

We ask God for all things, that we might enjoy life. God gave us life, that we might enjoy all things and a good start for enjoying life is to humble yourself to the vast grandeur of your surroundings. Get up early in the morning sit on the front porch as the sunlight begins to thaw the evening chill, smell the early morning dew, listen to the birds and at that special time of the year observe God's artwork as he paints the leaves of fall. You may find that sharing these happenings with your best friend and soul mate often makes them more pleasurable. Experiencing these many things can be very emotional but in most cases they will heighten your perceptions and increase your energy and vitality. To experience and enjoy these perceptions in life is to always keep the phone lines of your mind open to nature's call, by being grateful for your blessings. Don't keep the lines busy by always concentrating on work and physical things. Keep your life's answering machine message loud and clear that you are busy enjoying life's blessings. If doubt and anxiety or fear attempt to call they will get the message that you are busy and well on your way to knowing God. With this new determination and enlightenment getting to know your Lord is within easy reach.

Thoughts to Ponder

- Enjoy the journey, enjoy every moment, and quit worrying about winning or losing.
- Fill your life with as many moments and experiences of joy and passion as you humanly can. Start today with one experience and build on it.
- Heartache can crush your spirit but a loving heart can make the spirit cheerful.
- If your capacity to acquire has outstripped your capacity to enjoy, you are on the way to the scrap-heap.

"When people go to work, they shouldn't have to leave their hearts at home."

—Andrea & Donnie Murphy

I have always heard that you should find a job you love and you'll never have to work a day in your life. Wouldn't it be nice to love your job that much to wake up looking forward to having a great day at your work place every day? Being content at work takes a little more than just finding a job you like. It actually means becoming the right person with the right attitude and heart by personal choice, each and every day. At home it may be easy to start the day with a positive outlook. But taking that great to be alive attitude through breakfast; the commute, the parking lot and to the job at times may be a huge challenge. So no matter what happens between your wake up and the work place, your having a good or bad day will be heavily influenced by how much of your good heart makes it to work with you. A good heart strives for excellence at work because to know how to do something well is to enjoy it. A good heart plans on success rather than worrying about failure and keeps a positive perspective between work and play. The heart knows the more it wants something done well, the less it's called work and when a good heart is hard at work it doesn't know whether what it is doing is work or play. So wake up; get out that positive attitude, look in the mirror and smile but don't leave that good start and heart at home.

Thoughts to Ponder

- "Far and away the best prize that life offers is the chance to work hard at work worth doing."—Theodore Roosevelt
- Nothing is really work, unless you would rather be doing something else.
- When you find joy in your work you will have found the fountain of youth.
- A day of worry is more exhausting than a day of work.

"Whoso diggeth a pit shall fall therin."
—Proverbs, 26:27

When you are as bored today as you were yesterday and you are no longer imaginative in solving your life's situations, the big dig for the bottomless pit has begun. Complacency, boredom, the same dull routine, doubt, pessimism, lack of ambition are just few of the shovels that help dig the pit. Pitfalls will enter your life and are inevitable but don't make them a refuge or a reason for a continuous pity party. If they become a persistent way of life the pit may become a chasm much to large to overcome. Accept the challenge of climbing out of the pit that you have fallen into and dig your way out before it's too late. When you begin your struggle don't be shy, face them head on and approach them as if they were your opportunity to shine. Don't consider the possibility of defeat; in fact don't even think about defeat. Be persistent in overcoming them, as there are no problems as resilient as the human spirit. And even though your first attempt at digging your way out may not get you everything you want, not trying doesn't get you anything. You'll never know if you can overcome complacency, boredom, doubt and pessimism and what you are made of until you accept the challenge and try and try and try again.

Thoughts to Ponder

- Failure not to overcome the situation is easier to explain than failure even to attempt it.
- Your decisions determine your destiny.
- Attempt the impossible in order to improve on your position.
- Courage calls to courage everywhere, and once its voice is heard it cannot be denied.

"Until you value yourself, you won't value your time. Until you value your time, you will not do anything with it."
—M. Scott Peck

Someone once told me, "It's better to be prepared for an opportunity and not have one than to have an opportunity and not be prepared." Do you value your time? What's it worth to you? Will there be a tomorrow; are you curious about it? What will you be doing with it? They say curiosity killed the cat but my mom suspected me! It's important to value your time and let your curiosity propel you into adventures for today, tomorrow and next week. Ask yourself, "When will I go on that trip, when will I try to ride a four wheeler or a jet-ski?" or "Should I go to that movie or read that book I've heard so much about?" If you value your time then make plans or attempt to fulfill that curiosity and go for it. Be curious always! Knowledge, happiness and fulfillment will not acquire you; you must acquire it. Millions saw that apple fall but only Newton asked why. Curiosity is one of the permanent and certain characteristics of a healthy and vigorous mind. Don't say you don't have enough time. You have exactly the same number of hours per day that were given to Helen Keller, Pasteur, Michaelangelo, Mother Teresa, Leonardo da Vinci, Thomas Jefferson, and Albert Einstein. So value yourself by using your time with a curious mind. Use it wisely! Shoot for the stars and be curious!

Thoughts to Ponder

- You will always lose 100% of the shots you don't take.
- Do not wait; the time will never be "just right." Start where you stand, and work with whatever tools you may have at your command.
- If you strive for big results you must have big ambitions.
- Remember your Lord entrusted you with yourself.

> *"The movement from certainty to uncertainty is what we call fear."*
>
> —Jiddu Krishnamurti

Certainty in life, whether it is financial or romantic, is something all of us want or seek at one time or another. However, when you think you have found it, it is not all that it is cracked up to be. Certainty in life can bring contentment or piece of mind, but it can also have liabilities such as monotony, stagnation, boredom and possibly depression. In reality the uncertainties in life are the experiences that prove to be exciting, challenging and interesting and they keep boredom at bay as well as spark creativity. Yet it is the uncertain we have a tendency to dread and avoid. Fortunately or unfortunately for us the Lord made uncertainty the simplest thing in the world and certainty the most complicated. He gave us enough variation (uncertainty) in life to keep us from being bored and what do we want and look for? Certainty! with all it's liabilities. The world gives you challenges, adventures and worries to deal with each day and it's up to you to overcome the fear of the these unknown's by challenging them without fearing them. Here's to hoping you can understand the gift of uncertainty; face it, overcome it and delight in it—do not fear it!

Thoughts to Ponder

- Life is a process of becoming; a combination of states we have to go through.
- Where people fail; is that they wish to elect a state and remain in it. This is a kind of death. ~Anaïs Nin
- I think the thing that makes life possible is intolerable uncertainty; not knowing what comes next.
- Fear is that little darkroom where negatives are developed.

> *"Show them that we love them, not when we feel like it, but when they do."*
> —*Tom & Judy Martin*

It has been said that you cannot hold a torch to light another's path, without brightening your own. Your torch may well be the care and interest you have for others coupled with a smile of approval. Demonstrating your interest in those around you shows that you care about them and their situation. It also will brighten up their day and strengthen your kinship especially when it is unexpected and sincere. The demonstration of uncalled for love leads to healthy relationships and it has been proven that a healthy relationship is one of the most important factors in improving your happiness. The nice thing researchers have discovered is that when you feel close to those you live and work with you are four times as likely to feel good about yourself. But they also caution that you don't win at relationships, you win by having relationships. One of the biggest things blocking the light of your love is the shadow of being hesitant, so stop talking and start acting on showing them you care.

Thoughts to Ponder

- Surround those around you with optimism and optimistic attitudes. Look for the silver lining and spread good vibes and uplifting thoughts.

- Relationships are fragile things and require as much care as any other fragile and precious things.

- What better way to show your appreciation than to tell someone how important they are and how much you care? Start today!

- There'll be two dates on your tombstone and all your family and friends will read'em, but all that's gonna matter is that little dash between'em!

"If you don't run your own life, somebody else will."
—Marlo Martin

Choose to be positive, choose to be happy and choose to control your life; but by all means make sure the choices are yours. Having faith, taking control of your thoughts and especially associating yourself with happy people is essential in determining your happiness and destiny. Once you start making these decisions for yourself daily, they will become habitual. Choose to avoid negative and unhappy surroundings and feelings because people who are unhappy accept defeat in bad situations and then enlarge them and use them to predict an ominous outcome. Facts show us that eight out of ten unhappy people interpret the world in a negative manner and that eight out of ten happy people interviewed interpret the world in a positive manner. Happy people choose to explain away bad experiences as isolated incidents that have nothing to do with their abilities other than providing them with learning tools for future encounters. Just remember the "happy life" loves to be taken by the lapel and told, I am with you kid. So let's go! Choose who and what will influence your life!

Thoughts to Ponder

- Wherever you are, whatever you do, try to make a difference and if you're not sure what to do, choose to be positive.
- The old saying states, "Whether you believe you can or you believe you can't, either way you're right."
- Don't write yourself off; remember, if you don't believe in yourself, you won't be able to function.
- May your life be like a roll of toilet paper—long and useful and don't take life too seriously, your not getting out alive!

"If we have not peace within ourselves, it is in vain to seek it from outward sources."
—*Francois de La Rouchefoucauld*

There's an old Eskimo proverb that states "May you have warmth in your igloo, oil in your lamp, and peace in your heart." Finding that peace within ourselves becomes easier when you can acknowledge it has a direct relationship with your spiritual and religious beliefs. Studies have shown; regardless of what religion you affiliate yourself with, if you hold strong spiritual beliefs you typically will be satisfied with life while those who do not are typically unsatisfied. All the holy prophets conclude that you are here for giving not for getting and that you are here to serve, not to be served. I have found it is the attitude with which you do things that will determine the inner peace you receive from doing them. Doing good deeds with selfish desires or thinking of only ones self will often make your world a lonely place. But when you do for others in an unselfish way, the world will take on a touch of Heaven.

Thoughts to Ponder

- Good deeds with selfish desires will at best be a temporary fix.
- Life's greatest grief's we cause ourselves.
- Thinking that good deeds alone will bring you inner peace is like thinking that good deeds alone will get you into Heaven.
- Madison age 7 "Love's greatest gift is when Mommy gives Daddy the best piece of chicken."

"Coming together is a beginning. Keeping together is progress. Working together is success."
— *Ronny & Shirley Martin*

People often say, "I'm a self made man." But in the real world it's pretty difficult to succeed on your own or achieve total autonomy or independence. Is self-sufficiency an illusion? Even Thomas Edison was quoted as saying after questioned about his 21 assistants, "If I could solve all the problems myself I would." We are taught to resolve problems systematically with logic and reasoning and most of us, it seems, can handle earth-shaking conflicts better than simple interpersonal ones. Schools are so busy teaching science and technology they neglect or downplay the cultivation of sensitivity, responsibility, and commitment to other people or to their environment. When teaching technology and how to succeed why are they not also teaching the essentials for survival; such as reaching out to others or working together with trust? A few classes in goodness, gentleness, giving, caring, loving and spirituality as electives might also help. Surely science and technology mixed with some of these ingredients would lead to progress and ultimately success by coming together, keeping together and working together.

Thoughts to Ponder

- Synergism is the simultaneous actions of separate entities which together have greater total effect than the sum of their individual effects.
- Casey Stengel, "Gettin' good players is easy. Gettin' 'em to play together is the hard part."
- Coach Dean Smith to Michael Jordan in his freshman year at UNC. "Michael, if you can't pass, you can't play."
- Give the world the best you have and the best will come back to you.

"Most people are about as happy as they choose to be."
—*Abraham Lincoln*

I've heard that the happy people of this world are the people who get up and look for the circumstances that they want, and if they can't find them, make them. The best helping hand that you will ever receive is the one at the end of your own arm.

So think about how you want today to develop for you and then remind yourself that it's me who decides its development and its outcome. You can watch things happen, you can wonder what happened or you can choose to make things happen. My preference is the latter and hopefully yours is too. Remind yourself not to waste time thinking of the things you didn't get, can't have or don't have. Most important is not to worry about what you have compared to what others have. A number of studies and surveys have shown that: (1) Happiness is up to you, (2) The self-assurance you have makes up three-quarters of your happiness, (3) People are just as likely to be happy whether they have the most or the least of the things they want. (4) And that if a person really likes what they have they are likely to be twice as happy as those who have just anything they want. Choose it or loose it, happiness is up to you!

Thoughts to Ponder

- Happiness can be missed because it is dressed in overalls and looks like work.

- When something happens to you, good or bad, take the time to consider what it means.

- You can't go back and make a new start, but you can start now and make a brand new ending.

- When you focus on your family, the needs of others, your work, meeting new people, and doing the very best you can, happiness will find you.

> *"The real man smiles in trouble, gathers strength from distress, and grows brave by reflection."*
> —*Thomas Paine*

There are many kinds of smiles, each having a distinct character. Some announce goodness and sweetness others soften by their lingering tenderness and others brighten by their spiritual energy. People mimic the expressions of those around them, so a surefire way to influence them is with the way you express yourself. Sad faces evoke more sad faces and smiling faces evoke more smiley faces which ultimately improve positive communication. Smiles not only make other people happy they in turn make you happy. They cost you neither time nor money; they are magical and brighten your day and the days of others. As a special bonus smiles become a part of your personality and contribute to your beauty as your youth fades. As a part of your moral fiber, your smile represents your code of conduct, your standard of daily courage, discipline and integrity. Your smile can and will do a great deal in influencing those around you in putting on their happy face. Scientists have identified nineteen different kinds of smiles, each of them capable of communicating a pleasant message. Try one of yours today!

Thoughts to Ponder

- Remember, if your happy tell your face about it!
- I've learned that if you want to cheer yourself up, you should try cheering someone else up.
- Sunshine is to flowers what smiles are to humanity. These are but trifles, but, scattered along life's pathway their good is inconceivable.
- Before you frown make sure there are no smiles available.

"Nothing can stop the man with the right mental attitude from achieving his goal; nothing on earth can help the man with the wrong mental attitude."
—*Thomas Jefferson*

I've often heard that if you don't like something change it. If you can't change it, change your attitude and don't complain. At home or work rarely is it the big things that interfere with the growth of your relationships. The silly little things that should be just a cause for annoyance can grow to the point of becoming a real threat and grounds for irreconcilable differences. It's interesting how people can come together and join forces to overcome a major crisis in their personal or professional lives, yet, cannot handle little insignificant problems that confront them. Don't let trivial things end your relationships. As a group or as a couple or on your own, approaching difficult situations with a negative attitude will not help your chances of success but with a positive attitude you cannot help but to succeed. Every now and then you need to do an audit, face up to your little pet peeves and acknowledge that they are just minor flaws in the big picture. Once recognized as such, applying the correct attitude can smother out the sparks of doubt and discontent before they become the raging fires of failure. Try an audit today!

Thoughts to Ponder

- Positive thinking and enthusiasm together will help determine what you do about problems.
- List your little pet peeves and develop a habit of thinking about those things constructively in order to improve them.
- A successful relationship is not a gift. It is an achievement.
- Be positive and before you decide to put on a frown, make absolutely sure there are no smiles available.

"This is the day which the Lord hath made; we will rejoice and be glad."
—*Psalms 118:24*

How about you, do you delight, rejoice and feel the gladness of where you are in life and are you content with it? Researchers say that a large portion of your personal joy is dependent on the number and closeness of your friends, the closeness of your family and the type of relationships you have with them. They say that together they account for about 70 percent of your personal happiness. Try not to convince yourself of your joy and happiness with the thought of how many toys you have, where you live, how nice your home is, the car you drive, your large salary or by how much you have in the bank. It may have bought you a house but not a home, a bed not sleep, a clock but not time and your money cannot buy peace of mind nor heal a ruptured relationship or build meaning into a life that has no meaning. Ask yourself daily, how close am I with my loved ones and friends not how much stuff do I possess. Circumstances can take away your material possessions or your health. But no one can take away your precious friendships. So don't forget to make time and take the opportunities to make friends everyday. There is no greater treasure than a good friend and the pleasure, joy, and love that come from that friendship. Money and stuff might be useful but friendship and closeness with your loved ones and friends is essential in rejoicing and being glad.

Thoughts to Ponder

- Did you know the best things in life are not things?
- He who dies with the most toys is nonetheless dead!
- Your Lord didn't promise days without pain, laughter without sorrow, sun without rain, but he did promise strength for the day, comfort for the tears and light for the way.
- You can't find any true closeness in Hollywood, because everybody does the fake closeness so well.

> *"The good news is that the bad news can be turned into good when you change your attitude!"*
> —*Robert Schuller*

When life has you down and personal problems appear to be unsolvable try to resort to your faith; and your friends. It's easy to say; this will pass and tomorrow will be better, but there comes a time when you have to face up to your problems and hopefully not with a bad outlook or alone. It's also easy to say that you can alter your life by altering your outlook and attitude but without help the bad news can appear to be an insurmountable task. Always remember that the message of your faith is the good news and it means if you accept this news then your change of mind and acceptance of hope will bring about a change of attitude. Now the good news is the bad news is easier to overcome with your faith and accepting your friends help in the healing process. In any case sharing experiences with your friends can help you gain perspective and find solutions to problems that would otherwise be unsolvable. Remember it's easier to accept advice about building and developing your self-confidence, changing your attitude or having faith when others are there for encouragement. Reach out for help. It is a proven fact that people who interact and share with others feel better about themselves and feeling good about you is the first step in eliminating the bad news and turning it into good news.

Thoughts to Ponder

- What happens in you is more important than what happens to you.
- Not everything you face can be changed, but nothing can be changed until it is faced.
- Hope is hearing the melody of the future. Faith is to dance to it.
- Happiness doesn't depend on what you have; it depends on how you feel about what you have so remember one loyal friend is worth a thousand relatives.

"A friend is the one who comes in when the whole world has gone out."

—*Ralph Waldo Emerson*

Would you want a friend who changes when you change and who will nod his head yes when you nod? Heck! Your, shadow can do that! Friendship based on anything but your sincerity is bound to be empty and when you miss the moment to be a friend that opportunity is irretrievable. People say true friends must always hold hands, but true friends don't need to hold hands, in fact some cases they don't see or communicate for months or years but they know in times of need they are there for each other. So be a friend when you are needed not when you feel like being one! Good friends are hard to come by so when they are in need take the time to help, comfort, or just be with them. When you see the chance to go that extra mile for your friend, go that extra mile, the highway won't be crowded. In their hour of need don't walk in front of them, they may not follow; don't walk behind them, they may not lead; walk beside them and be their friend. Friendship multiplies joys, divides grief, understands our silence, is sympathetic and like a fine time peace beats true for all time and never runs down. Being a true friend will result in having a better feeling about yourself and an even closer relationships than you could have imagined.

Thoughts to Ponder

- Friends and wine should be old.
- No matter the circumstances appreciate your friends.
- Did you know the blessing of being an old friend is that you can afford to be stupid with them?
- The reason a dog has so many friends is that he wags his tail instead of his tongue.

> *"A man must be obedient to the promptings of his innermost heart."*
>
> —*Robertson Davies*

What does your innermost heart really want and will you be realistic in setting goals to attain it? If you expect nothing, then why are you apt to be surprised when you get it? And if you have great expectations; be sure to set attainable goals. In other words set yourself up and put the odds in your favor for success. People find themselves unhappy in life when they set unreachable goals for themselves because that's what they are, unreachable. There is a definite correlation between reaching goals and happiness and surveys have shown that people who set goals with high standards and reach them are no happier than people who set modest goals and meet them. Maybe it's time to re-evaluate yours! The more realistic and attainable goals you set the more likely you will feel good about yourself when you achieve them. When striving to achieve your goals remember that prayer and faith will enhance your inner strength and power to triumph. It doesn't matter what others say or think, only what you say and think and when you are down and out, keep reaching into your innermost heart. If you listen to and are obedient to the innermost prompting of your heart you will be amazed at the power within you to succeed.

Thoughts to Ponder

- What you prepare for is what you are most likely to get.
- The Lord has given every person the choice to be the architect of his or her own future.
- Happy people don't get everything they want, but they want most of what they get.
- If you ask a question you could be a fool for two minutes; don't ask the question and you're a fool for the rest of you life.

> *"Success based on anything but internal fulfillment is bound to be empty."*
>
> —*Martha Friedman*

I once read that to be successful in life, to be happy with where you are in life with internal fulfillment, you need to know whether you are burning up or burning out in your efforts to achieve your goals. With burn out you do things and worry about what others see; this is often described as "Out-sight". But when you do things for your own internal fulfillment and not for others; this feeling may be thought of as being burnt up, but in the process of burn up you gain insight into yourself described as "Inner sight." An easy way to check for internal fulfillment is to take a power nap. If you wake up with a feeling of fatigue and have no desire to light the way for others, you are burnt out. If you wake up with your battery charged and ready to resume your activity with zest and zeal, you were only burnt up. In conclusion you need "Inner sight", which includes; being creative, making work fun, doing things for your own internal fulfillment and not for others and then sprinkle your efforts with an occasional power nap. I would add that internal fulfillment not only breeds success but also breeds happiness.

Thoughts to Ponder

- Taking a nap is not only a good diagnostic tool it is good medicine.
- Some people live in a dream world, some face reality and those with "Inner sight" turn one into the other.
- In your quiet time just appreciate the fact that you are here, and to know that a Higher Power is with you and to trust It without fear.
- God had great insight when he made man before woman. It gave man a chance to think of an answer for her first question.

"You remember what people say when they are sick? That after all, nothing is pleasanter than health. But then they never knew this to be the greatest of pleasures until they were ill."

—*Hospice Pastor Jay Eastman*

Do you remember what you may have said or felt when you were last sick, sad or heartbroken? How great it was when you were; carefree, cheerful, and you were in love with life. You never realized then what it would be like without those greatest of pleasures until sadness or illness came your way. Remember when you become ill, feel hopeless and develop the fever of sadness; never loose your faith and hope. The ability to hope and have faith allows you to face the trails of daily life and look forward to better days. It reminds you that no matter what happens you can prevail.

There is no medicine like hope, no tonic more powerful than the belief that every trauma has a solution and that hope does indeed spring eternal. It takes hard and persistent work to develop this prescription for recovery but for those who do; the road to recovery will be shortened.

Thoughts to Ponder

- Every patient carries her or his own doctor inside.
- Health is not valued till sickness comes.
- Character cannot be developed in ease and quiet. Only through experience of trial and suffering can the soul be strengthened, ambition inspired, and success achieved.
- If you trust Google more than your doctor then maybe it's time to switch doctors.

> *"To reach the port of paradise we must sail sometimes with the wind, and sometimes against it, but we must sail, and not drift, nor live at anchor."*
> —*Oliver Wendell Holmes*

What's important in life is not so much where you stand, but to know in what direction you are moving and where you want to be tomorrow. Each and every one of your days is filled with accomplishments and good deeds but you need to be able to recognize them, enjoy them and share them. Life without good deeds or striving for daily accomplishments is like living life in a windless port at anchor. Why not begin rowing a little or keep some wind in your sails? There's a saying which goes something like this: "Bread cast on the waters comes back to you." Your good deeds of today and their influence on others may benefit you or someone you love at the least expected time. If you never see the deed again at least you will have made the world a better place and best of all your good deeds will get you a little closer to the port of paradise or that heaven of bliss you seek. After all, isn't that what life is all about? Your good deeds will bring even greater joy and happiness than that of the previous day. When you begin to take pleasure in the serenity of a smooth sailing moment it's ok to enjoy them; but not for to long!

Thoughts to Ponder

- Ralph Waldo Emerson, "Don't be to timid and squeamish about your actions. All life is an experiment. The more experiments you make the better."
- Accomplishments and good deeds give your life strength but in moderation gives life its meaning.
- Life does not give us chances. Life gives us chances to give.
- My dog has taught me to be a better person. One of forgiveness, giving love, being appreciative for kindness, goodness and living in the moment

"Life isn't about finding yourself. Life is about creating yourself."

—*Mal & Betty Mastel*

Some say total absence of humor renders life impossible. So each day when you are "Finding the real YOU," add some enjoyment and a little fun by always trying to put a little humor and laughter into your life. Young people seem to frolic and have fun all the time, why can't you? When the opportunity comes for a quick moment of joy and amusement then just do it. Why can't you just accept whatever comes your way, face it with courage and always try to look for a lighter side? Even at work your work ethic should be your enthusiasm with a little fun! Surveys indicate having fun and being jovial is a central factor of a satisfied life. It's a fact that when humor crops up, all our irritations and resentments slip away and a sunny spirit will take its place. People who can joke and have fun on a regular basis are 20 percent more likely to be happy on a daily basis and 36 percent more likely to feel comfortable with their age and stage in life. Mixing hard work with a little cement may be difficult but it may just make the difference between a day of depression with a little self-satisfaction and a day of celebrating life. Life is tough enough but if you have the ability to laugh at it you will also have the ability to enjoy it.

Thoughts to Ponder

- Create a happy day; have a little fun, be a little silly and make someone smile.
- My dog is worried about the economy because dog food is up to $3.00 a can. That's almost $21.00 in dog money.
- Humor is just another defense against the universe and using it like a rubber sword will allow you to make a point without drawing blood.
- Saw a sign in a restaurant window the other day that read, "Don't stand there and be hungry, Come on in and get fed up."

"Without trust, truthfulness and thoughtfulness, how can we feel love and understanding for another person?"
—*Jimmy & Theresa Murphy*

People work extremely hard at getting all the money and possessions they want in life but often fall short in their efforts in engaging happiness and seeking love. Is that special something missing in your life and do you only dream of being happy?

How often do you procrastinate when it comes to seriously pursuing a meaningful relationship? The real question becomes how do you go about understanding or nourishing your inner self-love and expand your capacity to experience true love? If you are clueless on how to begin and it seems to be impossible; remember in reality it's as basic as the, "A, B, C's" of nutritious eating habits. Begin the nourishment with the 3 supplements or 3 "T's" of a meaningful relationship that of trust, truthfulness and thoughtfulness. Success will only come about as a result of your efforts. So begin your nourishment journey with a first little step of trust, in truthfulness and thoughtfulness. Accept those modest achievements and know with modest success you can move forward with larger steps. And as you practice being truthful, trusting and thoughtful your soul will gradually begin to mature, you will slowly become happy with yourself and your capacity for love will automatically increase. Don't be afraid of growing slowly in the pursuit of self love; be afraid only of standing still.

Thoughts to Ponder

- It has been said "You can't have a meaningful love for another until you love yourself."
- When you are happy with yourself others like you more, you have better relationships and in turn become happier.
- Keep in mind that very few successful relationships would have reached the point of true love without the 3 "T's."
- You must let go of the "status quo" to grow.

> *"Our lives improve only when we take chances—and the first and most difficult risk we can take is to be honest with others and ourselves."*
> —Brad & Kassandra Rosewitz

New situations and demands in your life sometime requires decisions other than your casual insincere consent and just because you love someone, it doesn't mean you have to say yes all the time. In many of life's situations it becomes more difficult to say "No" to those you care for. It seems at times when their demands are wild or frustrating it is easier just to say "Yes." Do you want to tell them the truth, or the little white lie that will make you and them happy? In many cases your help and permissiveness only enables them to act in the same way they have been and makes you into what is called an enabler. There are times when being honest and saying no can be your greatest act of love. Being honest and Saying "No" will allow you to discover resources you never knew you had and it will help you experience the dignity that comes from being sincere and having been true to yourself. Your straightforward unequivocal "No" can also free you from the resentment you feel as the result of having been manipulated. This new awareness will allow you to feel a new sense of joy with yourself and lower your feelings of resentment, frustration, agitation and self-anger. The new found freedom will make your life magical.

Thoughts to Ponder

- When you believe in something with all your heart…stand up…speak out…make your voice heard.
- Look your loved one in the eye and say what you really think, don't just smile at them and say what you think they want to hear.
- Mark Twain, "When in doubt, tell the truth."
- Honesty is the best policy, but insanity is a better defense.

> *"What lies behind us and what lies before us are tiny matters compared to what lies within us."*
> —*Rocco & Sylvia Fumi*

I as stood before the full-view mirror I wasn't happy with the image I saw there. A older fat person with thin grey hair had swallowed up my whole body! But guess what? When my sweet heart walked into the room, gave me a hug and whispered an 831 "I-love-you" in my ear. WOW! - I love you, 8 letters, 3 words, 1 meaning! My forever friend thinks that I'm still attractive and the extra pounds and thinner hair have not dampened the feelings of love. Because of those eight letters the thick body and thinning gray hair were no longer important and what mattered is what was within me. My sole mate appreciated and valued me, therefore I felt more beautiful, lovable and loving. What a blessing the Lord placed in my life! Regardless of the changed appearance I suddenly realized I was happy to be where I was in life and I was happy to be me. It was not my ear she whispered into, but my heart. It was no my lips she kissed, but my soul. Whether you are a proud husband or wife, father or mother or a grandfather or grandmother; always remember that being encouraged by another to appreciate what lies within you is one of the greatest gifts you can receive, or give.

Thoughts to Ponder

- Your love will awaken something in them that they may have forgotten.
- Believe in yourself to regain confidence.
- The best and most beautiful things of this world can't be seen or touched. They must be felt by the heart.
- The older you get, the tougher it is to lose weight, because by then your body and your fat are really good friends.

> *"For myself; I am an optimist—it does not seem to be much use being anything else."*
>
> — *Sir Winston Churchill*

How often do you let other people's pessimistic nonsense change your mood? And how often do you take their glumness or meanness and spread it to other people at work or at home? Do you let a bad driver, rude waiter, curt boss, or an insensitive family member ruin your day? As their anger and pessimism builds up, they need a place to dump it. And if you let them, they'll dump it on you. When this happens, it is time to say "I'm not going to allow it anymore!" So just smile, wave, wish them well, let them pass you by and then move on. The secret to an optimistic outlook on life is how quickly you can re-focus on what's important to you. And what's really, really important is your influence on those whom you love. Don't allow your influence on family and friends to be that of skepticism or disparagement, always provide them with optimism and a caring attitude. The bottom line is; do not let doubt and distrust or pessimism take control over your day but rather choose to be an optimist because it makes no sense to be anything else but optimistic. And guess what? you'll be happier when you do!

Thoughts to Ponder

- When you are an optimist you are foolish enough to believe the best is yet to come.
- Your optimistic vision will become clear only when you look into your heart. He who looks outside; dreams and he who looks inside, awakens.
- Never underestimate the impression you may make on others.
- When someone shares with you something of value, you have an obligation to share it with others.

> *When I stand before God at the end of my life, I would hope that I would not have a single bit of talent left, and could say, "I used everything you gave me."*
> —Rev. Dick Cannici

Life is beautiful and to fully appreciate it you should dream whatever you desire to dream, to go wherever you wish and to seek what you desire. Sharing those dreams, desires and your happiness is a God given talent to be used throughout life's journey. One of the most precious things you can do with your talent is share your happiness with those who look to you for encouragement as well as those who have left a mark on your life, who make you laugh, who show you compassion when you were down have encouraged you to be positive. Hold them in your arms and let them know that one happy moment of love or joy with them can erase all the suffering that life has to offer. Share your happiness in every which way possible. Don't hoard it. Don't dole it out like a miser. Spend it lavishly like a millionaire intent on going broke.

Thoughts to Ponder

- When someone shares with you something of value, you have an obligation to share it with others.
- Do not hide your talents, they were given to you to use. After all, what good is a sun-dial in the shade?
- Life is about the gift not the package it comes in, it is what we make of it, it always has been, and always will be.
- You are successful when you get up in the morning, go to bed at night and in between you share your happiness with others.

> "To accomplish great things, we must not only act, but also dream' not only plan, but also believe and use the most powerful spiritual weapon we have—Prayer."
> —Patricia Murphy—Martin & Dennis Martin

With your dreams desires and plans always add prayer specifically focused on those dreams and aspirations. Continue to be thankful for what you have. Be creative. Be innovative. Think differently, positively, avoiding the negatives but always remember your prayers as being the most effective spiritual weapon when desiring to accomplish your dreams. Your spiritual weapon of prayer should be supported with positive planning and persistence, faith and the belief that you will get the best results in the battle with that prayer. The overall arsenal for accomplishing great things now consists of your goal and plan of action mixed with your weapons of persistence, positive thinking, patience and your stealth weapon and the ace in the hole, PRAYER. Just as in war all weapons must be used with deliberate aim; not just with a vague aspiration for success, but for specific goals in your plan. You may never succeed in this campaign, but whether you succeed or not, all of the weapons are yours to use. Keep in mind prayer is essential, everything else is secondary and achievement depends upon your faith in your prayers, remembering always; success will be on His time table not yours.

Thoughts to Ponder

- May you not forget the infinite possibilities that are born of faith!
- Sorrow looks back, Worry looks around, but faith looks up!
- When you think "I can't do it" God says: You can do all things (Philippians 2:13)
- When you think "It's impossible" God says: All thing are possible (Luke 18:27)

"If you think you have given enough, think again. There is always more to give and someone to give it to."
—*Norman Vincent Peale*

Everyone on earth has a purpose in life with many reasons for celebrating life. Expressing yourself in a positive way not only affects your loved ones, but affects the people around them. Your love and caring goes far beyond your immediate family and is now no longer a private affair. Like a pebble thrown into a pond, every action you perform spreads out in ever-widening circles. Your acts of caring and loving are not private but have the power to change the lives of the people we love and the people they love. Celebrate your life by being extra thankful and by giving all you can give of your positive upbeat side.

Thoughts to Ponder

- We were all born with a positive attitude; you learned how to be negative!
- Keep in mind that you are the most important asset you will ever have.
- Your positive attitude produces a positive perception and will change your situation for the better.
- Are you aware of the fact that no husband has ever been shot while doing the dishes?

"When your life is filled with the desire to see the holiness in everyday life, something magical happens: Ordinary life becomes extraordinary, and the very process of life begins to nourish your soul."
—*Rabbi Harold Kushner*

Your personality is not your physical entity, but is, in fact, made up of everything about you that is not physical. Your values, attitude, as well as your memories, desires, fantasies, and sense of humor make up your personality and are the essence of your soul. Since it is not physical, it cannot get sick, it cannot die, it cannot disappear, and, I suppose, it is immortal. And yet your soul needs nourishment! Nourishment sometimes comes when you are simply in awe of your natural surroundings and you have that feeling of the presence of a greater being. At other times, you get that rich feeling when you forgive someone, give to charity, participate in acts of kindness, compliment others, study, and pray. When you do these things, something inside tells you, *Yes, this is how I should feel*. It's kind of like a rush of happiness feeding your soul, and the ordinary life becomes extraordinary.

Thoughts to Ponder

- Did you know that a smile is one of the most inexpensive ways to improve your looks?
- Few things are harder to put up with than the annoyance of a good example.
- You cannot choose how you feel, but you can choose what to do about it.
- Life is short, so forgive quickly. Believe slowly. Love truly. Laugh uncontrollably. Never regret anything that makes you happy. And have a wonderful journey!

"If you could choose one characteristic that would get you through life, choose a sense of humor."
—*Jennifer Jones*

Did you know you were born with everything you need to be happy? And since you were born with nothing, you can be happy without physical things. If "things" could make you happy, the Lord would have given you money, a new car, a fancy suit, or a boat at birth. Instead, you were blessed with many talents and, throughout life, the free will and opportunity to develop them. In either good times or when life is dealing you a bad hand, being able to find a little humor in them and being able to focus on your blessings is essential. Being grateful and staying motivated is much easier if you can keep a sense of humor. When you can find humor in the smallest, largest, and in-between problems in life, you will be able to find the motivation to get by them and the ability to celebrate being alive. When this happens, your smile will be continual, and the road of life will be less bumpy.

Thoughts to Ponder

- You may not always be happy, but you can always share happiness.
- The burden you carry will be lightened when you laugh at yourself.
- Listening to children is like shopping in the bargain basement: you get lots of things you didn't know you needed at a very good price.
- Are you aware that it's useless to hold a person to anything they say while in love, drunk, or running for office?

> *"Every day I live, I am more convinced that the waste of life and loss of happiness lies in the love we have not given, the powers we have not used, and our selfish prudence that will risk nothing."*
>
> —Mary Cholmondeley

In giving of our love and doing kind things unselfishly for others, happiness can be found. It's almost effortless to leave a trail of love and happiness because it's painless, uncomplicated, and doesn't cost much. Some of the happiest people are those who give thanks by doing little things, such as written thanks to friends or coworkers, and by showing small sincere gestures of appreciation. At work, do not only thank the individual who lends a hand, but also let others know how thankful you were for the help you received. Give some encouragement "out of the blue" or show someone you care and are appreciative that they are in your life. You can utilize cards, letters, telephone calls, or e-mail messages. In some cases, hugs work! Don't waste your life by not using your God-given gift of giving love. It is a requisite part of happiness that one is willing to give and share. The good news is that when you give and share, the source of your replenishment will never run out. Love given is love gained.

Thoughts to Ponder

- Happiness is a function of accepting what is, and it becomes a way station between too little and too much.
- To go without some of the things you want is an essential part of happiness.
- Instead of saying, "I don't have the time," take a moment and send one letter or make one call.
- Parents' and grandparents' love comes straight from the heart.

"Nothing is worth more than this day."
—Johann Wolfgang Von Goethe

Wouldn't it be nice if people thought about you when they didn't have to? Think about it! When you're sick, the flowers and cards are nice, but generally you are not in the mood. Wouldn't you forgo some of those gifts on birthdays and holidays for a surprise card or phone call during the year? These feelings go both ways, and thinking about others when you don't have to is a sign of true friendship. The next time you think, *I should call so-and-so or send a card to a friend,* maybe you should. Offerings of thankfulness and demonstrations of love cannot and should not wait for your convenience or their sickness. Don't procrastinate and wind up saying, "I meant to get that gift or say thank you—who would ever have thought that person would be taken from me so suddenly."

Thoughts to Ponder

- Isn't it fascinating to know friendship is like good health? Its value is not known until it is lost.
- The will to act now is the first step in victory.
- If you can't be a good example, then you'll just have to be a horrible warning.
- Today is the day for men and women everywhere to exercise that decision to live lovingly and to demonstrate thankfulness.

"Where you find no love, put love, and you will find love."
—*John of the Cross*

You often hear about people who remain in stagnant relationships, settling for discarded crumbs of love, and then rationalizing: "This is like a prison, but that's how life is." Trying to avoid surprises, not attempting new and intuitive ideas, and taking no risk with love is another way of locking yourself up in a prison of stagnation. In order for love to succeed, you must take charge of your situation not by being passive, but by responding with a positive "can-do" attitude. When you accept the responsibility for creating and maintaining a meaningful love, the results will be empowering and include an inexhaustible supply of love to give as well as increased awareness of the happiness in you and within those around you. When you can give and win at love, it feels as if nothing hurts. You cannot fail if you stay receptive and believe that all things are possible with that love.

Thoughts to Ponder

- Did you know that most unhappy people are those who fear change?
- If you want to fail, try too hard. If you want to succeed, try hard enough.
- You create your own fate, but most of your failures are directly traceable to your own behavior.
- If you fear less, hope more; eat less, chew more; whine less, breathe more; talk less, say more; hate less, love more, then your level of happiness will increase.

"To do good in the world, you must first know who you are and what gives meaning to your life."
—*Paula P. Brownlee*

Do you know in the entire world there is no single person exactly like you? As a result of your uniqueness, everything you produce is authentically yours. As you increase your self-awareness, there will be things you don't understand about yourself and many things you may or may not like about yourself. But these are not grounds for disliking yourself because your dreams, fantasies, hopes, behaviors, and abilities are yours alone, and they give meaning to your life. They are your makeup and determine who you are, what you can become, and give meaning to your life. As you are discovering and enhancing your self-awareness, you can't help but become more thankful for the gifts you have been blessed with. You may never entirely know yourself, but never cease trying because that's what allows you to give meaning to the world.

Thoughts to Ponder

- Knowledge will come with experience, but wisdom has a tendency to linger.
- Anything you learn in this world is never wasted.
- Your worth is determined by the good deeds that you do, not the fine emotions that you feel.
- Grandparents are builders of dreams and sculptors of souls.

"The less of routine, the more of life."
—*A.B. Alcott*

Sometimes in our daily routine we get so wrapped up in our own situation that we ignore and forget that our loved ones and coworkers exist. When routines become so mundane and you find yourself becoming more considerate and understanding of total strangers than of your coworkers and spouse, it is time to make a change. A friend told me he carried around a rubber band to remind him to be flexible at times like this. It didn't always work, but when it did, altering his daily routine just a little bit was almost like having a new life. Even though you think they know it, simply say thank you to your fellow workers, spouse, children, and parents today. A kind word, sincerely stated, can work magic. Try it; you never know, it may rekindle magic back in your life where the magic has vanished. Remember, there's no precisely "right" moment to express those thoughts that are hidden in your soul.

Thoughts to Ponder

- If you can't change your fate, change your attitude.
- You have to take it as it happens, but you should try to make it happen the way you want to take it.
- Dream deep and remember, every dream precedes the goal.
- Why do they call it a television set when you only get one?

"When life is filled with thankfulness of everyday life, something magical happens: ordinary life becomes extraordinary and the very process of life begins to nourish your soul."
—*Rabbi Harold Kushner*

If life is boring, dull, and lacks enthusiasm, it may be time to refocus your inner thoughts and nourish your soul. To nourish your soul means you need to be thankful for everyday life. It also means being able to reflect, focus, and be thankful for the good things that have taken place in your past. The thoughts can be used as stepping stones in the nourishment process of your attitude. When your attitude begins to shift from indifference to one of thankfulness, you will know it, and it will help carry you to the next phase of the procedure. Take a minute to reflect on a happy moment in your life. Revisit a past blissful experience that vividly remains with you. Visualize and experience it again, see it again, hear the sounds, and feel the sensations. What in that experience stays with you and what from that experience are you thankful for? Re-discovering thankfulness will bring back feelings of fullness, a joy of being alive, and a new awareness about your good fortunes. You will also find that thankfulness begets thankfulness.

Thoughts to Ponder

- No matter how old you get, if you can keep the desire to be creative, you're keeping the child in you alive.
- You can't build happiness on what you intend to do!
- Nourish your soul by being thankful.
- To keep a true perspective on your importance, you should have a dog that will worship you and a cat that will ignore you.

"Conditions are never just right. People who delay action until all factors are favorable do nothing."
—*William Feather*

This is so true not only at work, but also in your personal life. If you are waiting to ask the boss for a raise or to tell your spouse something special, do not wait for an ideal circumstance or what you consider to be the best opportunity. Chances are, they will never come. There are two ways to face your present situation: First, you can either alter the difficulties by procrastination, or you can alter yourself by taking action and facing them. Half the failures in life's travels are due to pulling in your reins just before leaping for that dream. Before you know it, the opportunity and the point of no return has passed you by. If you don't ask or act, how will you ever know? What are you waiting for?

Thoughts to Ponder

- Did you know the first gift given to you was life, love the second, and when you begin to understand them, you will have received the third?
- No matter the conditions, it's okay to change your mind, but always take time to laugh every day.
- By perseverance, the snail reached the ark.
- Close your eyes—remember and visualize the following: cops and robbers, cowboys and Indians, kick the can, and sitting on the curb.

"Though every hello is the beginning of a goodbye, do not lose heart, for every goodbye may also be the beginning of another hello."

—Anonymous

All of your experiences throughout life and everyone with whom you have made contact with make up the blend of paint with which you have been painting your life's portrait. Each moment of every day you are brushing, etching, modifying, and creating that portrait. You become a part of all those you have met and said hello and goodbye to. On the pallet from which comes your portrait, you can always add a new hello. It is never too late to renew friendships or make new ones; step outside of your comfort zone by visiting new places, joining that fellowship group or professional organization, or doing volunteer or outreach work. Start new adventures with a big hello and create the most colorful portrait of yourself possible. Among your most prized possessions should be the word hello. And when it is time to say goodbye, don't cry because it's ended; smile because it happened.

Thoughts to Ponder

- By living your life one day at a time, you live *all* the days of your life, so don't miss any of them by living in the past or the future.
- Do not give up when you have something to give. Nothing is really over until the moment you stop trying.
- When God measures a man, He puts the tape around the heart instead of the head, and so should you.
- Remember, the grass may look greener on the other side, but it still has to be mowed.

"Can anything be sadder than work unfinished? Yes, work never begun. "

—Christina Rosetti

"You can be anything you want to be," "You can succeed at anything you set out to accomplish in life," and "If you desire something strongly enough, it is yours for the taking" are all statements you have heard before. Solutions come from need and desire, but they do and will not materialize on their own. Only with the willpower to follow your desires with positive actions can you improve on or succeed at your work and personal relationships. The question is, do you really want it badly enough to do the soul searching and hard work needed to acquire it, or are you just kidding yourself? When you begin your journey, have faith and hold that desire with a singleness of purpose. Even if you failed or cannot complete the mission, it is better to have tried than not!

Thoughts to Ponder

- It doesn't matter how much cash you have because wisdom is purchased on the installment plan.
- If you try to be somebody by being like everybody, you will end up being nobody.
- Knowledge comes by way of ignorance; therefore, you ought to be encouraged by what you don't know.
- The early bird may get the worm, but the second mouse gets the cheese.

"Time is like a river—it flows by and doesn't return."
—Chinese Proverb

As you get older, it seems like the river of time moves faster and faster. Aging is not anticipated with thoughts of pleasure, and most of us do not look forward to the process with a positive and happy attitude. Aging is an activity of attitude and mind, and a positive attitude is essential for that peace of mind. You grow older faster when you give up having fun and no longer get excited by the new or when you resist change, relinquish hope, and cease to revel in the game of life. Let's not do that, but rather live up to the old saying, "You are only as old as you feel and act." Start enjoying and start celebrating the richness of the world around you. Believe in yourself, and hear the laughter in the acts of love that surround you. Seek the fountain of love and the fountain of youth, because as long as you can live, love, and laugh now, you will remain young.

Thoughts to Ponder

- A man travels the world over in search of what he needs and returns home to find it.
- Don't spend your days stringing and tuning up your instrument. Start making the music now.
- If you feel that your life is on hold and time has passed you by, have faith and remember that He is waiting with you.
- The best way to touch someone with your love is by hugging. In return you strengthen your arms!

"We could never learn to be brave and patient, if there were only joy in the world."

—Helen Keller

When you are down and out, things are not going your way at home or work, and you are wondering if that right person will come into your life, stay busy, be brave, and most of all be patient. Be brave and be patient because just around the next corner that "Mr. or Miss Right" could be there for you. Don't fret. Tomorrow things will be better at work, and when you get home the family will greet you with a huge smile and a hug. If you are going to get emotional exercise, don't get it from jumping to negative conclusions. Since you cannot predict the future, you should get your emotional exercise from drawing positive conclusions from today. Have faith, be brave, be patient, think positive, and you will get positive results. Remember the little engine that could, that said, "I think I can, I think I can."

Thoughts to Ponder

- When you've cried so long and your heart is in anguish, try to remember there is Someone who is counting your tears.
- Why didn't anyone ever tell us that cheerfulness is the daughter of employment?
- Be patient and life will give you a second chance.
- Don't just give your children and grandchildren good advice; give them good memories.

"To be successful, the first thing to do is fall in love with your work."

—*Sister Mary Lauretta*

Most people say that in order to be happy and content with life, to have positive personal relationships, improved work ethic, and success, you need to love your job. In today's world, loving your job is at best difficult, but if you are one of the lucky ones, then bless you. Moving from saying, "It's just a job," to liking it and even loving it is not an easy task. You can move in that direction by having faith, trust, some self-love, and a sense of where you are headed. With a positive attitude about oneself and those around you, it becomes easy to love life and, in turn, enjoy your work. Like a circle, as you begin enjoying life, your personal actions will reflect and reveal your inner feelings, and your work will become enjoyable, as will your life. Being successful means accepting all of the positives of your environment starting with yourself, friends, and co-workers, and then using them to your advantage.

Thoughts to Ponder

- Excellence comes in the pursuit of perfection, not its achievement.
- If suddenly your outlook is brighter and you find traces of hope, maybe Someone has whispered to you.
- Rather than walk this earth lightly, walk firmly with determination and leave your mark.
- Gotta love your job and pay; did you know that one hundred years ago, a competent accountant could expect to earn $2,000 per year, a dentist $2,500 per year, a veterinarian between $1,500 and $4,000 per year, and a mechanical engineer about $5,000 per year?

"Look your troubles in the eye. Problems not faced do not go away. Life is a rollercoaster of ups and downs. Anticipate each dip and prepare for it."
—*Rev. Joseph Maron, S. J.*

When the ups and downs of life come your way, how do you cope with them? Do you face them, or do you just turn away and ignore them? Some people turn to meditation, formalized religion, or chants, while others retreat into themselves or lash out in anger. In many cases, your support can come from "soul mates," which can be friends, spouses, coworkers, or even children. Others read books, go to movies, take some educational classes, or spend more time with nature. Both may provide the answers you need. No matter what your circumstances, your heart will always provide some of the answers. Remember, the lowest points of life are where you sometimes learn the most valuable, magical lessons for moving on to happiness.

Thoughts to Ponder

- Rather than focus on the thorns of life, smell the roses and count your blessings, giving thanks for each of them.
- When you have pains, try not to be one.
- Until you have peace within yourself, you'll never be content with what you have.
- Have you ever wondered why there are flotation devices in the seats of planes instead of parachutes?

"To accomplish great things, we must dream as well as act."

—*Anatole France*

When you think you are failing to achieve your goals, it's always easier to blame past situations and decisions for your inactions of today. In reality it may be the way you are reacting to your present situation, and it may do well to examine your current attitude and behavior. Having a "pity party" filled with indifference, anger, weakness, or ignorance contributes to giving up control of your life. Take action and regain control by putting anger, sadness, and regret behind you. It's okay to feel anger with pain and disappointment, but it's not okay to stay angry. It's okay to mourn the closing of a chapter in your life, but it isn't okay to mourn the rest of your life. It's okay to regret all the things you could or should have done differently, but it isn't okay not to forgive yourself. Don't let your anger today spill over into tomorrow, but rather look back without regret and go forward with positive dreams and anticipation.

Thoughts to Ponder

- Did you know you make your own attitudes and habits, and then your attitudes and habits make you?
- Just think how happy you'd be if you lost everything you have right now—and then got it back again.
- Happiness may elude you, but if you focus on your family, the needs of others, your work, meeting new people, and doing the very best you can, happiness will find you.
- Getting old, being a parent, and being a grandparent isn't for sissies.

"All human wisdom is summed up in two words:
wait and hope."

—*Alexandre Dumas Per'e*

Have you ever had visions of the perfect relationship? Do you envy the relationship that you think your best friend has? You know the one that appears to have a special connection without conflict and appears to be overflowing with tenderness and understanding. People sometimes waste their time comparing their hopes and desires with what others have by searching, wishing, and hoping that their relationships could be as wonderful. They feel they have a right to happiness and true love immediately. Why should they have to wait and hope while others have it now? Guess what? All they have is unhappiness! If you asked what they were really searching for, they probably would have no idea, and, in fact, they probably would not be content until they married themselves. Patience and hope and realizing there is no perfect love, only human love, will make you be able to appreciate the love you have. Maybe you are happier than you thought.

Thoughts to Ponder

- You need to open your heart and eyes to see that opportunities to help and serve are everywhere.
- Somehow when you know your faults are thick, you begin to realize that your love is thin.
- When nothing makes sense and you are confused or frustrated, there is a Higher Power to turn to.
- I wonder why they sterilize the needle for lethal injections.

"Thoughts are energy, and you can make your world or break your world by thinking."

—*Susan Taylor*

At times it may appear that other people get all the breaks. They are climbing the ladder of success, you are stuck on the first rung, and you think you do not have total control of your life. In reality so much of what happened may have been avoidable had you thought about it longer or differently. If you had taken control of your thoughts and directed those thoughts and energies positively, the problems would not appear to be so insurmountable. Learning to cope with your innermost feelings means making attitude adjustments a part of your daily life. This is a skill you can develop, but it takes practice and persistence. Here is something to think about: Though others have more money, beauty, and brains, when it comes to the rarer spiritual values such as charity, self-sacrifice, love, honor, and nobility of heart, you have an equal blessing. Thus by choice and directing your energies, you can be the most beloved and honored person you can be. It's simply attitude.

Thoughts to Ponder

- I've learned that when you want to cheer yourself up, you should try cheering someone else up.
- What a fool does in the end the wise man did in the beginning!
- "The longest way 'round is the shortest way home," "Make haste slowly," and "Haste makes waste" are all homely proverbs with the same meaning.
- Do you think that when people asked George Washington for an ID he just whipped out a quarter?

"Life is a festival only to the wise."
—*Ralph Waldo Emerson*

In personal relationships, some people expect to receive from their partner the equivalent amount of love and effort that they give. Wow! Are they in for some big disappointments! The joy and happiness you attain is not based on a formula of "I did this" or "I did that, therefore I should receive X amount of satisfaction from my good deed." It's not a "what goes in comes out" kind of world when it comes to love. And love will not be dispensed to you in equal measures of what you did or didn't do. Becoming wise about love includes the acceptance that we all have different weaknesses, strengths, possibilities, histories, resources, and knowledge. You may think it possible and desirable for two people to completely balance each other and give equally in a relationship, but don't plan on it. The reality is you may have to give more or work harder in the relationship to make it successful. Life can be a festival, but remember that imbalances create the challenges and motivation that make true love.

Thoughts to Ponder

- Love cannot be wasted. It makes no difference where it is given; it always brings in big returns.
- Isn't it sad that there are people who love you dearly but don't know how to show it?
- Love your own soul, comfort your heart, and, especially, remove the self-pity from yourself; self-pity has killed many!
- Going to church will not make you a Christian any more than going to the local hamburger joint would make you a hamburger.

"A man's indebtedness is not a virtue. His repayment is. Virtue begins when he dedicates himself actively to the job of gratitude."
—*Ruth Benedict*

For what do you have to be thankful? Think about the last few days and how wonderful most of your experiences and blessings were. A few might include your car, home, boat, spouse, family, friends, or your bicycle! You should be grateful for those things, but as you grow older and more worn, your gratitude should include much more. Each morning give thanks and be grateful for your sight and hearing, for a mind that is intact, and for the fact that you can ride a bike, go swimming, and take long walks. Eventually, you will come to understand what really is important to you in your walk through life. A Sunday school teacher of mine once said, "Let's rise and be thankful, for if you didn't learn a lot today, at least you may have learned a little. And if you didn't learn a little, at least you didn't get sick. And if you did get sick, at least you didn't die. So the least you should be is thankful."

Thoughts to Ponder

- When you were younger, why didn't someone teach you that when you act as if you are happy, it tends to make you happy?
- Children find comfort in flaws, ignorance, and insecurities similar to their own. Love your parents for letting you see theirs.
- Pursue thankfulness by never letting adversity get you down, except on your knees.
- To his dog, every man is Napoleon; hence the constant popularity of dogs.

"Have you ever tried to make someone love you? It's next to impossible! You have the power to give away love and to love other people, but to make them love you is difficult. To do so you must change the kind of person you are, thus changing the kind of world that you live in."
—Unknown

Seeking to be loved is a challenge similar to finding the butterfly of happiness. The harder you try, the more evasive the butterfly. Stop and slow down and it may just land on your shoulder. It has been said that everyone loves a happy person, but love, like happiness, is always a by-product of whom and what you are, not of what you do. You don't make yourself happy by chasing the elusive butterfly of happiness; you make yourself happy by being a good person. The happy and loved people I know don't think about being happy; they just live their lives by being a kind neighbor, a good friend, and a caring family member. If you think about others, happiness will just kind of sneak up on you while you're busy doing good. Always keep in mind that love and happiness come as a reciprocal process.

Thoughts to Ponder

- Are you aware that if you take thirty minutes every day to relax, breathe, and laugh at yourself, it adds years to your life?
- Look at life through childlike eyes.
- Never doubt when you are in the dark what the Lord has told you in the light.
- Love is what's in the room with you at Christmas if you stop opening presents and listen.

"The human spirit is stronger than anything that can happen to it."

—George C. Scott

How true this quote is. In addition to studying the book *The Desert Fox* by the German General Rommel on desert tactics for tanks, General George Patton must have studied the Bible. First Corinthians 10:13 says, "No temptation has seized you except what is common to man, and God is faithful; he will not let you be tempted beyond what you can bear. But when you are tempted, he will also provide a way out so that you can stand up under it." Reading this verse was the answer given to General Patton to solve a special problem. It may comfort you to know that everyone—no mater how rich, educated, or sensitive—has problems, makes mistakes, agonizes, and at times loses faith and stops trusting in him or herself. Even with strong spiritual beliefs and faith, people can always use human encouragement. Your concern and gentle encouragement can build confidence, promote growth, ease the burden of stress, and help others to regain their self-esteem. A kindness you can show in time of need and a word of encouragement at the right moment can and will work magic.

Thoughts to Ponder

- When you act to elicit the best in others, you bring out the best in yourself.
- Become so wrapped up in something that you forget to be afraid.
- You need to have faith and doubt, but they need to be working side by side to take you around that unknown curve.
- I think that people who keep dogs are cowards; they haven't got the guts to bite people themselves.
-

"Whether you think you can or you think you can't, you are right."

—Henry Ford

If you think you can keep a positive outlook on life, you can. On the other hand, if you think you can't influence your outlook on life with your attitude, you can't. When you are feeling low or very negative, try being thankful for all the bad things that aren't happening to you. Your pet didn't get run over by a car today; you don't have Alzheimer's disease; your kids haven't pierced their tongues; and the hurricane went the other direction. Disastrous events by virtue of not having struck can be a great mood elevator, and the higher degree of outrageousness, the better you will feel about your blessings. There is no limit to what you can accomplish in life, but your attitude is essential for your personal growth and happiness. Thankfulness coupled with hard work, a belief in yourself, and optimism will always enhance the chances of reaching your goals. With a new, positive, and healthier outlook on life, you gain an extra—it's called self-respect.

Thoughts to Ponder

- Did you know that one man with courage makes a majority?
- In the face of uncertainty, there is nothing wrong with hope.
- If you haven't got all the things you want, be grateful for the things you don't have that you don't want.
- No one appreciates the very special genius of your conversation as your dog does.

"The only preparation for tomorrow is the right use of today."

—Unknown

Are you passionately involved and totally wrapped up in enjoying and loving life? Do you love the transformations of the seasons, the variety of color, and the spring rainfall? To see, hear, walk, and to be able to lie on your back and look at the stars or enjoy music and paintings are the things that make up everyday miracles. Many of your peers are "yawning" their way through life with seemingly nothing left to be excited about. Some of them envy children's enthusiasm for life and yearn for the "good ole days." It is not necessary to revert to childhood days to rekindle your eagerness for life. Try finding some joy in the commonplace things of life and savor the excitement and joys in each and every moment of the day. You may just find that this will reignite your enthusiasm for life and remind you that there is still very much living and loving within you.

Thoughts to Ponder

- Sometimes we are so busy adding up our troubles that we forget to count our blessings.
- Did you know the soul would have no rainbow had the eyes not tears?
- Instead of using the words, "if only," try substituting the words "next time."
- Find joy in knowing that even though it may seem difficult to go on, the morning's joy will soon dispel the darkness.

"You will know them by their fruits."
—Matthew 7:16

Actions speak loudly! Your outside images are a reflection of what is going on inside of you. You are what you do, and what you do is a reflection of your thankfulness, spirituality, and your gratitude of life itself. If you love life, there will be tangible evidence of love in your actions. Don't wait for a brush with death, a car accident, or a cancer experience to awaken your sense of thankfulness. Do you need a close call to appreciate the amazingly wonderful fact that you are alive, breathing, and enjoying the world through your senses? Thank the Lord for the goodness of being alive on this awesome earth in your healthy body at this time. Thankfulness for being able to smile at a stranger or caress a loved one can be the best feeling you will ever have and the ultimate joy of living. It could possibly be the best feeling you have in your human repertoire. Keep in mind, your fruits are your reflections!

Thoughts to Ponder

- Life affords no greater responsibility, no greater privilege, than the raising of the next generation.
- Faith, hope, and love together will help you raise children with positive attitudes in a negative world.
- Your dog is your friend, your partner, and your defender. You are his life, his love, and his leader. He will be yours, faithful and true, to the last beat of his heart. You owe it to him to be worthy of such devotion.
- Reveal yourself by letting your fruits be seen as your heart swells with thanksgiving.

"Today let me be aware of the treasure you are. Let me learn from you, love you, and bless you before you depart. Let me not pass you by in quest of some rare and perfect tomorrow. Let me hold you while I may, for it may not always be so."
—Mary Jean Iron

There is a special awareness you feel about your vulnerability immediately after sickness, a close call in your car, or a breakup with your sweetheart. It wakes you up to the wonder of your existence and pulls you out of your complacency with life. "Awareness Practice" can help you through troubling times. It can help you to appreciate and enjoy the everyday or common events in your life. And to develop it, you need only to pay special attention and be thankful for what you are doing now—not what happened to you yesterday or that quest for the perfect tomorrow, next year's vacation plans or the dinner plans for next week. Try concentrating on appreciating the miracles of the ordinary. This may include playing with the children, conversing with you spouse, noticing his or her new haircut or the twinkle in his or her eyes. Just acknowledging or sharing in their joy of achievement and accomplishment is a tremendous booster of self-esteem. In time and with practice, you will become keenly aware of those blessings and treasures you value most in your loved ones.

Thoughts to Ponder

- Open your heart to the beauty that surrounds you.
- Did you know love is the first feeling you feel before all the bad stuff gets in the way?
- Catch and kiss your blessings as they fly by, even in the midst of sorrow or suffering.
- As a grandparent, you can tell you grandchildren hundreds of "true" stories, whether they happened or not.

"If you want to be successful, it's just this simple. Know what you are doing, love what you are doing, and believe in what you are doing."

—*Will Rogers*

When you know, when you love, and when you believe, the smile on your face will disclose it. And when you smile the whole world smiles with you, just as when you give the world the best you have the best will come back to you. There is a very real relationship between what you contribute and the results you get out of this world. There is no such thing as a "self-made" man. In reality you are the sum of thousands of others. Your character, thoughts, and success are made up of the kind deeds others have done for you, the words of encouragement received from others, and the adjustments you have made to their advice. Just as knowing, loving, and believing leads to success, being thankful, having faith, and keeping a grateful mind in realizing you couldn't have done it alone will help sustain that success.

Thoughts to Ponder

- Clinging to the patterns you know will inhibit your ability to discover what you don't know.
- Be sure the love you take is at least equal to the love you give.
- Deciding to have a child is a momentous decision. It is to decide forever to have your heart go walking around outside your body.
- The greatest mistake you can make in life is to continually fear that you will make one.

> *"I was always looking outside myself for strength and confidence, but it comes from within, and it is there all the time."*
>
> —*Anna Freud*

If you take away surprise and mystery from your life, life can become dull and boring. Boredom is an indicator that you have lost your motivation or your focus on what's important for your success and happiness. Leaning on others for motivation is not always the answer and at times can be a mistake. Friends can encourage you, but I believe the only person who can motivate you is you, and since that inner strength is already there, why not use it? Plus, it's free! To stay self-motivated you need the desire to attain your goals, a real belief that you can succeed, and a clear image of yourself achieving them. No matter who you are or what your age, remember that real motivation comes from within, and if you want it bad enough, you can motivate yourself to get it.

Thoughts to Ponder

- Since the future is where you will spend the rest of your life, make a confident choice to look forward to it.
- Did you know that joy is the standard of your heart when your Lord is in residence there?
- Decide to stay focused and motivated on reaching your goals rather than concentrating on problems you might have in reaching them.
- Madison, age seven: "When you love somebody, your eyelashes go up and down and little stars come out of you."

"You cannot be friends upon any other terms than upon the terms of equality."
—*Woodrow Wilson*

When you and your friends care for each other because of your differences and not in spite of them, you've truly found forever friends. We are all individuals, similar to others in many ways, but in many ways different. Accepting those differences allows us to grow, to change, and, with time, to develop long-lasting friendships. When friends change, don't forget; each one of us is distinct, and we are also in a state of continual change of growing and learning. The "Equality Factor," or the knowledge and acceptance of our individuality and equality, is the characteristic that allows us to attract and make new friends. Have faith, treat others for what they are, not for what you want them to be, and ask yourself, *Am I a forever friend?*

Thoughts to Ponder

- Faith goes up the stairs that love has made and looks out the window that hope has opened.
- Reach out and touch someone. People love that human touch, holding hands, a warm hug, or just a friendly pat on the back.
- If you treat people for what they might be and might become, they will become their better selves.
- Did you know that grandkids and their grandparents get along so well because they often have a common simplicity?

"Our business in life is not to get ahead of others, but to get ahead of ourselves—to break our own records and to outstrip our yesterday by our today."
—*Stewart B. Johnson*

Every day, whether at home or at work, being true to oneself can be a very difficult task, and being honest, upfront, and open about how you really feel does not come easy. You may fear that in doing so, you will expose yourself to ridicule or rejection, so instead of being yourself, you take the easy path of acting nonchalant, playing sophisticate, or remaining aloof, hoping to protect yourself. By identifying with this unreal character, staying at arm's length, and being cynical, you can feel accepted or successful. So staying at an arm's length is not the answer to being true to oneself. No matter what the situation might be, the "real you" is superior to anything you can concoct. Being true to oneself begins with not being cynical about you and others, but rather in looking for the good in both. Don't be surprised if revealing the authentic you gains you trust and respect tenfold from others.

Thoughts to Ponder

- Did you know that self respect is the cornerstone of virtue?
- You can make someone's day! Send them a nice note.
- What lies behind and before you are tiny matters compared to what lies within you.
- Plan ahead. It wasn't raining when Noah built the ark.

> *"When you reach for the stars, you may not quite get them, but you won't come up with a handful of mud either."*
> —Leo Burnett

Children are extremely curious and enthusiastic about everything. Wouldn't it be nice to have their enthusiasm for life and endless energy? Can you recall personal feelings from childhood when you would lie on the grass watching a bug or looking up at the cloud formations passing overhead or wanting to touch the stars? You dreamt of future adventures with no cares or fears about failure. To pursue your dreams and to ignite your enthusiasm for life you need not revert to childhood. Reverting means to find joy in the commonplace things of life and finding adventure in each and every moment by loving its changes, its color, and its movements. You could be watching boats returning home with a beautiful sunset as a backdrop or enjoying a winter wonderland, music, or paintings but always remember to enjoy your friends. What have you done lately to light up your enthusiasm in reaching for the stars?

Thoughts to Ponder

- Aim higher than your reach.
- What counts is not the number of hours you put in, but how much you put in the hours.
- The only time in your life when you wanted to get older was when you were a kid.
- Remember good friends are like stars: you don't always see them, but you know they are always there.

"Think wrongly if you please, but in all cases, think for yourself."

—*Doris Lessing*

Having to make important decisions can sometimes be cause for grief, stress, and, at times, procrastination. The problem is how to remain true to you in this world of so many distractions? How do you stay balanced no matter what the pulling forces might be? The old saying goes, "When you get to the end of your rope, tie a knot and hang on." But when it appears there is no one you can trust or no earthly authority you may go to, always remember that with faith and prayer you can rely on your decisions. Hanging on to your faith and remaining strong means that you have to listen to the force of your inner authority rather than to the would-be experts. Think for yourself; the road through life may become bumpy at times, but hold on for the ride. It's all worth it!

Thoughts to Ponder

- Worry is like a rocking chair; it will give you something to do, but it won't get you anywhere.
- They say a man could retire nicely in his old age if he could dispose of his experience for what it cost him.
- Accomplishing your goals can be made easier when you trust in your own confidence and truly believe that you can accomplish them.
- Remember to be patient. In time, the grass becomes milk.

"If one asks for success and prepares for failure, he will get the situation he has prepared for."
—*Florence Shinn*

Some people have success, position, reputation, money, and a marriage, yet remain unhappy and neurotic. They attain outward success but have inner failure because they accept for themselves an inadequate or wrong attitude on life. The secret is to get rid of the attitude of "I might," "I think," and "I ought," and replace them with "I can," "I will," and "I must." Life, after all, is the sum of all of your positive as well as your negative choices. Unfortunately, some of us seek positive change outwardly yet subconsciously choose failure. Preparing for growth is your option, but it means waking up with a positive attitude, not remaining half asleep with illusions of failure. Faith will expand your spiritual horizon, and when coupled with a more optimistic and thankful personality and an attitude of gratitude, it will prepare you for true success.

Thoughts to Ponder

- Accept yourself just as you are, then you can change.
- Most of us would rather be hurt by flattery than helped by criticism.
- When you encounter setbacks and you are down and out, singing "Amazing Grace" can lift your spirits for hours.
- The sign on my plumber's truck reads, "Don't sleep with a drip; call your plumber."

"When you are expecting others to achieve success, the best service you can give to them is be silent, be patient, be hopeful, try to understand, and wait. The key to everything is patience."

—*Unknown*

To be successful in life, you have to be patient and encouraging to yourself and you have to be patient and encouraging to others as well. Easy to say, but putting these virtues into practice is sometimes difficult and requires a little faith. They can be demonstrated or put into action by offering clarity in what is expected, setting goals and deadlines, showing concern, and establishing milestones for yourself and others. When you provide a little encouragement, it helps eliminate procrastination, and, of course, recognition of any accomplishments will provide the inner strength needed for success. Demonstrating patience with that encouragement also helps one over the daily bumps and challenges of that highway called life.

Thoughts to Ponder

- Don't confuse your career with your life.
- Remember, the greater the obstacle, the more glory in overcoming it.
- Before success, entrepreneurs average almost four failures. This amazing persistence sets the successful ones apart.
- Did you know that when trouble arises and things look bad, there is always one individual who perceives a solution and is willing to take command? And, very often, that individual is crazy.

"Anyone who limits his vision to memories of yesterday is already dead."

—Lily Langtry

Have you ever imagined what would have been if you could have changed something in your past? Thinking about the "what if" is a waste of the present time. If you took time to examine your current position in life, it could be traced back to every decision you ever made. So since life is not a continuous smooth line, but a series of moments taking place now (your now-moments), don't waste too much time on memories and make it a priority to seize the now moment and live each and every one. You can't change the past, but when you become aware of the interconnectedness of your experiences, you will become excited about where you are now and all the gifts with which you have been blessed. Releasing the yesterdays of life allows joy, laughter, bliss, love, and beauty to fill your heart. You will have taken control of your life and clearly enjoyed some of the best experiences of your present life. Someone once said, "Enjoy yourself now; these are the good old days you're going to miss in the years ahead." Enjoy the here and now, such as laughing at yourself or running through sprinklers like a kid or midnight phone calls that last for hours or a sunrise stroll—or maybe you could just enjoy life for absolutely no reason at all.

Thoughts to Ponder

- When something joyful happened and you were filled with awe, did you know Someone had smiled down upon you?
- If you want the rainbow, you have to put up with the rain.
- As long as you are alive, you have the power to polish, re-cut, and place the precious jewel of yourself in new settings daily.
- As you grow older talk about your memories with love and the young will listen.

"He that wrestles with us strengthens our nerves and sharpens our skills. Our antagonist is our helper."
—*Edmund Burke*

At home and work, we sometimes shy away from disagreement and conflict in order to keep peace. Yet in many cases, these situations can be used for positive gains. There's an old saying that "change means movement, which creates friction. Friction will cause heat and in turn will cause controversy." It's easier to sail smoothly with those with whom we agree than to grow and advance with those with whom we don't. Always look for the positives that can result from conflict rather than the negatives.

Thoughts to Ponder

- Prevent controversy. "Listen or your tongue will keep you deaf."
- When you are tired and discouraged from fruitless efforts, do try to realize He knows how hard you have tried.
- If someone refuses praise the first time you offer it, they probably would like to hear it a second time.
- Ryan, age ten: "Love is like grandpa and maw who are still forever friends even after they know each other so well."

"Great minds have purposes, others have wishes."
— *Washington Irving*

At home or work, we all have some purpose. It could be professional success or it could be a loving relationship we desire. Someone once said, "Exceptional things have been achieved by he who dared to believe that something inside of him was superior to the circumstances." Being confident in yourself, enthusiastic, optimistic, persistent, and patient will allow you to convey your wishes into purposes and eventually accomplish great things. When you are expecting loved ones or coworkers to achieve success, the best service you can give to them is to have confidence in them and be encouraging, patient, and optimistic. Remember: having a great mind is when you can take your wishes, add purpose with a goal, and do it with optimism, enthusiasm, and patience.

Helen Keller said, "Optimism is the faith that leads to achievement. Nothing can be done without hope and confidence."

Thoughts to Ponder

- Don't run through life so fast that you forget not only where you've been, but also where you are going.
- Do you know that stumbling and falling is not the same as failing?
- Fall for someone who makes you smile, because it takes only a smile to make a dark day seem bright.
- Great things are not done by impulse, but by a series of small things brought together.

"Nothing in life is to be feared. It is only to be understood."
—Marie Curie

When searching for happiness, a great deterrent in finding it is the fear of venturing out of your comfort zone. Striving for personal success is scary to some of us, as it requires a change of attitude, trying something new, commitment, or just plain sticking out one's neck. It's always easier to take the easy path or to back off from commitment or to hide from others. Staying comfortable in your own little circle of safety, in "your space," it becomes easy to isolate yourself from the things that could give your life more joy and meaning. Don't allow the fear of change to deter your happiness; take a chance. Voices from the heart deserve to be heard and understood. So listen to them and take one little step at a time. Remember, where sincerity and love strongly exist, the apprehension, disappointment, and fears of change will be reduced to nothing.

Thoughts to Ponder

- Your mind is like your stomach: what is important is not how much you put into it, it is how much you digest.
- If you don't venture from your comfort zone, you will regret it because you can't build on it, and it's an appalling waste.
- Daylight savings time: why are they saving it and where is it kept?
- Andy, age seven: "At my first football game, I was scared. I looked at all the people watching me and saw my daddy waving and smiling. He was the only one doing that. I wasn't scared anymore."

"One nice thing about egotists: they don't talk about other people."

—Lucille S. Harper

Most of us have a little trace of egotism in our personality, but hopefully not a lot. We think we are good managers, supervisors, co-workers, and spouses, but fail to look outside of ourselves long enough to be a fair judge. To be good in these endeavors, we must first move the focus from self to others. Encouragement is oxygen for everyone's soul, and by not being demeaning but by helping others you both can realize your potential. If they succeed, you can find pride, and with their professional and personal growth you can feel self-satisfaction without boasting. When we share with and encourage others, we ourselves become wiser for it. And by the way, these are also the beginning steps to the understanding of love.

Thoughts to Ponder

- Take the first step in faith. You don't have to see the whole staircase, just take the first step.
- Remember, if you find yourself in a hole, the first thing to do is stop digging.
- As you ramble down the road, keep your chin up. Remember, the test of your character is how you behave when you don't know what to do.
- If you are fair to everyone, the people you expect to kick you when you're down will be the ones to help you get back up.

"A life lived in love will never be dull."
—Leo F. Buscaglia

Just because you may be hopelessly and totally in love does not mean you still cannot follow your own heartbeat. That's part of the wonder of love. Yes, you and your partner can still do some of the things you like to do, but everything does not have to be done with each other. Relationships are not weighed and dispensed in equal measures. Each person brings varied possibilities, strengths, and weaknesses to the relationship, some of which you share totally with each other and some you don't. These traits can either be nurturing or they can promote insecurity, depending on how you handle them. Remember that imbalance creates the challenge and motivation for growth.

Thoughts to Ponder

- Treasure those memories of the past and joys of the present by sharing them with those around you.
- Don't let a little dispute injure a great relationship, and remember that silence is sometimes the best answer.
- Enjoy the wonder of love by being a good listener. When you listen, you hear ideas different from your own. It's hard to share love when you are talking.
- Everyone needs a significant other because there are some things that can't be blamed on the government.

"A soul friend is someone with whom we can share our greatest joys and deepest fears, confess our worst sins and most persistent faults, as well as clarify our highest hopes."

—*Edward C. Seller*

In Walt Disney's movie *Anne of Green Gables,* Anne referred to her best friend as her "kindred spirit" or "soul friend." The most important things in life you can do for your children can be done within the four walls of your home. Sharing their joys, hopes, and dreams and letting them know you are there for them is essential. Parents can make the most significant of contributions by imprinting the awareness of and the development of "kindred spirits" or "soul friends" in their child's life. This will enable the child to grow up knowing long-lasting and true friendships. Most psychologists say imparting self-awareness, imagination, and a deep moral sense of what is right and wrong to your children will provide a basis for developing sound interpersonal relationships. This is something we all need to do!

Thoughts to Ponder

- The best type of relationship is one in which your love for each other exceeds your need for each other, and it is absolutely wonderful.
- You should always leave loved ones with loving words. It may be the last time you see them.
- You really shouldn't say "I love you" unless you mean it. But if you mean it, you should say it a lot. People forget.
- *Dogs love their friends and bite their enemies, unlike people, who are incapable of pure love, and it seems they always have to mix love and hate.*

> *"Thus shall you think of this fleeting world—a star at dawn, a bubble in a stream, a flash of lightning in a summer cloud, an illusion, a dream"*
>
> —Dr. D'Espagnat

The world is moving so fast that it seems that as you get older it is forever on fast forward. Especially during the happy times, it's as if you are aboard an express train picking up speed to your final destination, and no matter what you say or do the engineer driving will not stop or slow down. We used to sing, "Row, row, row your boat gently down the stream. Merrily, merrily, merrily, merrily, life is but a dream." Is it reality or a dream or an illusion when you feel pain or disappointment? Albert Einstein said, "It's okay to assume life is just a dream because, logically, there is no way to prove it isn't." Either way, when faced with a strenuous situation, you need to slow down and have patience and self-composure. Wanting actions, solutions, and answers now will cause you to make hasty judgments that could lead to suffering unnecessary pain and despair. Be it a dream, an illusion, or reality, learn patience, and accept the times of discontent along with the times of sublime joy. Many of your problems are just worries that disappear when you have the patience to find out.

Thoughts to Ponder

- Think about your destination. But don't worry if you stray. The most important thing is what you've learned along the way.
- What if your family, health, friends, spirit, and work were like juggling balls? Which one could you afford to drop?
- Learn from the mistakes of others. You can't live long enough to make them all yourself.
- It's hard to understand how a cemetery raises its burial cost and then blames it on the cost of living.

"Every day is my best day. This is my life, and I'm not going to have this moment again."

—*Unknown*

What a great attitude! I hope you have the same one. Don't wait until you become aware of your eminent death to decide to gain your real freedom in life. At work, at home, and at play, if you can't change your circumstances, you can still choose to be happy. Decide to go to work upbeat, positive, and happy; then just watch how many people around you will get happy too. Celebrate life, smile, and choose to be happy; you may be surprised at the results. Take advantage of your circumstances now; the chance may not come again. Your positive influence on someone will be your contribution of love to this earth today.

Thoughts to Ponder

- Have a perfect end to this perfect day, and I hope that every day is just as wonderful in its own way.
- If you don't have a sense of humor, you probably don't have any sense at all.
- The happiest people don't always have the best of everything. They just make the most of everything that comes their way.
- As you grow older, remember that unless you're made of cheese it doesn't matter.

"The love we give away is the only love we keep."
—*Elbert Hubbard*

Most of our frustrations and anger at home, work, or play are the result of wanting life to be different and more exciting. If you dwell on what you didn't get or want and continue with your negative attitude, guess what? Negativity! On the other hand, if you gear your attentions toward trust, love, and optimism, there's a good chance you can replace a negative attitude with a positive, loving one. The love and caring attitude you develop will determine the amount you can give to others. It's a well-kept secret, but you can never run out of love. As you develop the skills to trust, to listen, to be optimistic, and to love yourself, you will be amazed when you see your anger and frustration diminish. Spread some love; celebrate life daily by giving away some of that love you have been hiding.

Thoughts to Ponder

- Criticism of you by others isn't necessarily the truth—it's just someone's opinion.
- Many of the world's problems are caused by narrow minds and wide mouths!
- Remember, life may be tough, but you're tougher.
- Why do they call it "chili" if it's hot?

"I don't believe that life is supposed to make you feel good, or to make you feel miserable either. Life is just supposed to make you feel."

—*Gloria Naylor*

Do you feel like you have met or are with your soul mate? You will know when your measure of love is reached when you don't measure. Some say the chances are very rare that you'll meet the person you really love who equally loves you in return. I don't believe that to be true; in fact, many of us are with that forever friend now. You may think they don't care for you as much as you care for them, but maybe you are not appreciating what you have and maybe you are taking too many things for granted. At some point you should make it a priority not only to love them, but to appreciate them, because at any time they may be taken away. Once you meet that soul mate and forever friend, don't ever let them go. The chance might never come your way again to feel that way. As you get older, it is not the things you did that you often regret, but the things you didn't do.

Thoughts to Ponder

- We spend too much time looking for the right person to love or finding fault with those we already love when instead we should be perfecting the love we give.

- Did you know that hope discovers what can be done instead of grumbling about what cannot?

- You have no more right to consume happiness without producing it than to consume wealth without producing it.

- How to treat your soul mate: Hold them, cuddle, surprise and compliment them. Smile, listen, laugh, and cry with them. Romance them, encourage them, believe in them. Pray with and pray for them. Shop with them, give them jewelry, and buy them flowers. Write love letters to them and go to the ends of the earth and back again for them.

"Every single ancient wisdom and religion will tell you the same thing. Don't live entirely for yourself; live for other people. Don't get stuck inside your own ego because it will become a prison in no time flat."

—*Barbara Ward*

Life is going well; you are happy. You have a positive attitude, get through troubled times easily, you care for yourself and are spiritually content, but something is missing! There is a feeling of incompleteness in your life and you don't know why. Maybe you are selfish—an "I" person—and don't know it. Here is a tip: Share "you" with others; give them your love, help them as a friend, share your joy and happiness, be there for them, and reflect that inner joy for them to see. When you were young, you were taught to share. When did you forget? Those rules still apply. Share with those less fortunate, share your joy with those who need encouragement, share laughter with those who haven't heard any in a long time, share your tears with those who have forgotten how to cry, and, most of all, share your faith with those who have none. Practice on the outside what you feel on the inside and the results will be awesome, and that feeling of something missing in your life will disappear.

Thoughts to Ponder

- Live your life so that your children can tell their children that you not only stood for something wonderful, you acted on it.

- When you harbor bitterness, your happiness will dock elsewhere.

- Many people never get anywhere in life because when opportunity knocks, they are in the backyard looking for four-leaf clovers.

- Giving of yourself, or sharing "you," with others will keep you from becoming trapped in loneliness.

"It's kind of fun to do the impossible."
—*Walt Disney*

It's fun to get yourself in hot water as long as you come out cleaner for it. Everything worthwhile is a risk. Think about it. Would you be where you are today if you never took a risk? Remaining in your comfort zone and playing it safe will not bring you success, and when you stop taking risks, you miss the point of the game of life. Risk brings with it the possibility of failure and pain; however, the greatest and most lasting pain of all will come from the emptiness you will feel from never having risked. Saying, "I wish I would have—" is a terrible thought. No one has ever succeeded and done the impossible by staying home and playing it safe.

Thoughts to Ponder

- If you are successful, you will win some false friends and some true enemies. Go for the success anyway.

- Judge your success by what you had to give up in order to get it.

- Remember, if your Creator had a purpose in equipping you with a neck, He surely meant for you to stick it out.

- Why is it when you want a garment to shrink, it won't? And when you don't want it to shrink, it will come out of the dryer and fit your dog?

"The two things that fill my mind with ever new and increasing wonder and awe are: the starry heavens above me and the moral law within me."
—*Immanuel Kant*

Getting along at home, work, and play simply takes "doing unto others as you would have them do unto you." If we were to follow this faith-based moral law, it would create a basis for living together where you can agree, cooperate, adapt, compromise, and share. Instead of people saying, "What's in it for me?" they might begin with, "What am I able to do for others?" We are blessed with the starry heavens above just as we were blessed with the free will to share of ourselves. If our sharing means happiness, then giving others complements, encouraging them, spreading your joy, or maybe just laughing and talking with them could be a good start. Remember, every person you meet is fighting his or her own battle for love and survival and deserves whatever kindness you have to give.

Thoughts to Ponder

- *Always Say A Prayer* (ASAP): There's work to do, deadlines to meet, you've got no time to spare, but as you hurry and scurry, always say a prayer.
- In the midst of family chaos, "quality time" is rare. Do your best; let God do the rest; and always say a prayer.
- It may seem like your worries are more than you can bear. Slow down and take a breather; always say a prayer.
- God knows how stressful life is; He wants to ease our cares, and He will respond ASAP.

"There is no greater reflection of yourself than when the form or your behavior reflects and scatters joy and not pain around you."
—*Unknown*

Nothing is as fatal as predictability, and it is a reflection of your personality. Dull routines have a way of insidiously creeping into your life and determining your behavior. Sunday breakfast after church at the same restaurant, Wednesday bowling, Fridays with the in-laws, you know! The same old things over and over! To make that once loving relationship a prisoner of a mundane and predictable lifestyle is to take away its passion, allow it to wither, and possibly be lost forever. Change your behavior; spread happiness by trying a serendipitous act such as a surprise dinner, an unexpected gift, or a little craziness to shake up your habitual existence. The results will be astounding.

Thoughts to Ponder

- Don't take the things closest to your heart for granted. Cling to them as you would your life, for without them, life is meaningless.
- When you found out the joy you share with others circulates back to you, did it excite you?
- A loving atmosphere in your home is the foundation for your life. Do all you can to create a tranquil, harmonious home!
- Plant turnips in your garden today: turnip for service when needed, turnip to help one another, and turnip the music and dance.

"Every time you acquire a new interest or a new accomplishment, you increase your power of life."
—*William Lyon Phelps*

When was the last time you tried something new? Maybe it's time to move outside of your comfort zone and take that risk. Don't shy away from trying just because you feel you may fail at it. Making mistakes and not having all the answers is not a crime; not trying is. There is nothing wrong with not succeeding and making mistakes as long as you are willing to admit them and make an effort to strive for personal betterment. Aside from acquiring new skills and gaining experience, the reward for succeeding is that you have increased your power of life, self-confidence, and control of your destiny. If you think you know it all and are unwilling to try something new, guess what? You have no way of finding out that you don't.

Thoughts to Ponder

- Some people succeed because they are destined to, but most people succeed because they are determined to.
- The heart of a man cannot be determined by the size of his pocketbook.
- Living and working together would be easier if people showed as much patience as men do when they are fishing.
- Men are like fish. Neither would get into trouble if they kept their mouths shut.

> *"Man has the ability to change his life's attitudes and ways just by a mere conscious endeavor."*
> —Henry David Thoreau

Isn't it encouraging that you have the ability to improve a work situation or change a personal relationship just by a conscious effort, a compromise, personal adjustment, or a flexible action on your part? I'm sure you have heard or been told to be careful of what you repeatedly say because it's possible you can become what you say. So it only makes sense that you should be careful and make every effort to be as positive as possible as a means to control your life. Avoid saying things like, "I'm too old to change," "I can't," "I won't," "Well, that's just the way I am," or "There is nothing I can do about it." These dead-end statements accomplish nothing. Make a conscious endeavor to think positively, to verbalize positive statements, and to take control of your attitude toward life. When you do, maybe your life will evolve into the happy one you wish it to be.

Thoughts to Ponder

- The temptation of being negative, once yielded to, will gain power.
- Good and bad habits are first cobwebs, then cables.
- Remember, the foolish and the dead never change their opinions.
- Keep negative thoughts to yourself; the crack in the levy that lets a drop or two ooze out soon becomes a hole, which lets out a flood.

> *"Our memory is a monster; you forget...it doesn't. It simply files things away. It keeps things for you or hides things from you and summons to your recall with a will of its own. You think you have a memory, but it has you."*
> —John Irving

When you have an important decision to make, it is filtered by past experiences, good or bad. As you are about to make that final decision based on recent events, the memory monster returns. Those poor choices, bad experiences, and iffy decisions of bygone days decide to cloud up what was to be an easy resolution. And when you try to figure out what to do, without thought, your decision is influenced by what was. Never fear; knowing this should help alleviate the anxiety and help you use past experiences to your advantage. No one is permanently preprogrammed, and you have the ability to change by assimilating the old with the new and moving on without fear. Someone once said, "He who neglects to drink of the spring of experience is apt to die of thirst in the desert of ignorance." Taking this knowledge and using it positively can definitely influence your decisions in a productive way.

Thoughts to Ponder

- Age doesn't always bring wisdom; sometimes age comes alone.
- The measure of your character is not what you get from your ancestors, but what you leave your descendents.
- Worrying and complaining about your past experiences should be replaced with persistence at making your future journeys better.
- The nicest thing about the future is that it always starts tomorrow.

"Take a chance! All life is a chance. The man who goes the farthest is generally the one who is willing to do and dare."

—*Dale Carnegie*

Human behavior is unpredictable and volatile. Knowing this, you have no guarantees of a certain type of behavior from those at work, in play, and especially in your marriage or a romantic association. People grow; they gain new insights, change directions, and have changing needs, especially when daring to take on new challenges. Change is inevitable. So, rather than seeing the changes in your friends, coworkers, and lovers as some sign of an altered or weird personality, try to accept or even celebrate these changes as a new and undiscovered facet in them. Hopefully, they will do the same for you. Always keep in mind, "Predictability is a bore."

Thoughts to Ponder

- Those who bring sunshine to the lives of others cannot keep it from themselves.
- You never really find out what you believe in until you begin to instruct your children.
- Your mind can only hold one thought at a time. Make it a positive and constructive one.
- Do it today: pick up the phone, send that e-mail, write a letter, kiss your mom, or hug your dad.

"There is only one happiness in life, to love and be loved."
—*George Sand*

    You may love many people in a variety of ways, but you ultimately need to have that one special love. You will *know* when it happens. That one person in your life will be the one with whom you will have security, comfort, privacy, affection, and exclusivity. This special someone will be your soul mate to love and be loved by. Your bonds will bind you in mysterious ways both physically and emotionally, and in your private space you will have no ego problems, you will have great joy, great happiness, and feel no limitations. When you find that happiness in life, you will become one, but at the same time you will be two. When you love and are loved, you have truly found the secret to happiness in life.

Thoughts to Ponder

- To most people you might just be one person. But to those who love you, you might be the world.

- Love is a strange mixture of opposites: affection and anger, excitement and boredom, stability and change, restriction and freedom.

- Don't waste time looking for the perfect lover. Instead spend your time creating the perfect love.

- Take the time to enrich you life and eliminate boredom by sharing everything with your soul mate. Remember that complacency kills and love enhances.

> *"When laughter makes people glad that they are alive and more conscious of love, and when it lifts their sadness and severs them from anger, that is sacred."*
>
> —*Unknown*

Did you know your soul feeds on laughter and joy but will wither and die without them? Choosing laughter and joy should not be an indulgence, but should be considered an investment. So choosing to be happy and joyful should be a no-brainer. Start by making your choice daily, try it twice per day, and eventually you will have painted your heart happy. The process begins by doing the little things that you love on a regular basis. Read on your swing, take a walk in the park, chat with an old friend, work on a crossword puzzle with a loved one, light a fire or candle, listen to your favorite music, park your car at a scenic location and enjoy the view. You will be more generous and sensitive, and your joy will make you happy to be alive. To do so is sacred!

Thoughts to Ponder

- When you open your heart to laughter, all existence will appear naturally, beautifully, and harmoniously.
- When you wake up in the morning, check for a pulse. When you find one, smile, laugh, jump for joy, and go nuts.
- I don't want to work, but I have to work to earn enough money so that I don't have to work.
- The universe, by definition, is a single gorgeous celebratory event. Why not join in and celebrate your life today?

"When we give of what we have, we are ready to receive what we really need."

—*Douglas M. Lawson*

Did you know that the tools for you to become a happy, successful person are readily available, and it is never too late in life to become that happy person? Actually, it's really easy and rather simple. To begin with, ask yourself what things give you happiness. It may be a word of encouragement or praise, a hug, a smile, a warm greeting, or maybe it could be just a nod of acknowledgment from those you know. Once you know what makes you happy and have received them, it's your obligation to share and give those things back to your loved ones and coworkers. Everyone requires basically the same things for happiness and success, so you can hardly go wrong by giving them freely. It's a wonderful and simple way to share what you received and what you have. Start now!

Thoughts to Ponder

- Greed is often regretted; generosity—never.
- When you are at work, never admit that you're tired, angry, or bored.
- The poorest of all men is not the man without a cent, but the man without a dream.
- Make someone's day: pay the toll for the person behind you.

"Love is the driving force for the highest values of life."
—Pitirim Soroken

Some people believe that, along with innocence, love is the first wisdom given to you at birth and that all things are derived from that knowledge. It's easy to talk about filling your life with love, but what is that action we call showing love? Since there is no specific activity called "showing love," it must consist of some of those mundane things we do for others without thinking about them: playing a game with your child when you are dog tired, helping take care of someone at church who needs help, or even returning that wallet you found on the street. You usually don't plan on acting with love or showing love at any particular time of the day or put it on your list of things to do. But to become more loving, you have to listen to those little tugs of your heart. When you get those gentle urges, just listen to them, even if they are insane. When the opportunity to demonstrate love presents itself, you will know it.

Thoughts to Ponder

- Growing old is mandatory; growing wise is optional.
- Be a loving person by enjoying all you do today; compliment others on the way they look; share to your heart's content; and most of all, have a good laugh.
- You may be disappointed if you fail, but you are doomed if you don't try.
- Keep your relationship stimulated with a conscious effort at resolving problems, and the results will be a growing love.

"If you want the present and the future to be different from the past, study the past, find out the causes that made it what it was, and bring different causes to bear."
—*Will and Ariel Durant*

Each advancement or failure in life serves to prepare you for the things to come. Slowing down your pace and taking the time to examine and learn from your successes and failures will help make decisions for tomorrow much easier. Someone once said, "Let each one of us step to the music he hears, however measured or far away." So take one step at a time to discover your strengths and use them to your best advantage. If you plant positive thoughts from your past experiences in your mind, you will gain a harvest of good things. Pace yourself and allow each move forward to serve as an enhancement, with the past and present being used as the guide for your future. The positive things you think about you will become.

Thoughts to Ponder

- Your reputation is made in a moment, but your character is built in a lifetime.
- A handful of patience is worth more than a bushel of brains.
- Put yourself in another's shoes. If you feel that it hurts you, it probably hurts them too.
- Don't judge life by one difficult season. Persevere through the difficult patches and better times are sure to come some time.

"If I give all I possess to the poor and surrender my body to the flames, but have not love, I gain nothing."
—1 *Corinthians* 13:3

It appears the writer Paul is trying to tell you that love is not love unless you use it. Though the Scriptures the message of love is repeated. Second Peter 1:5–7 says, "For this very reason, make every effort to add to your faith goodness; and to goodness knowledge; and to knowledge, self-control, perseverance; and to perseverance, godliness; and to godliness, brotherly kindness; and to brotherly kindness, love."

What else do you have to give but love that costs you so little? What else do you have that is inexhaustible in supply? What else transfers the same benefits to the giver and the receiver as love? Unless we are always actively living in love, we are not utilizing the greatest gift we have been given. It's never too late to offer love.

Thoughts to Ponder

- Wonderful isn't it to know love lights more fires than hate extinguishes?
- Yesterday is a canceled check, tomorrow is a promissory note, but today is cash in hand. Since we only have today, spend it wisely.
- Where you find no love, put love, and you will find love.
- Be glad your Lord doesn't give you everything you ask for.

"Kindness and intelligence don't always deliver us from pitfalls and traps. There is no way to take the danger out of human relationships."
—*Barbara Grizzuti Harrison*

Loving relationships in life are some of the best things you have. Your personal relationships at home or at work cannot survive under constant verbal neglect but will if cultivated by expressions of tenderness and goodness. Even occasional kindness and intelligence will eventually wither and die without cultivation. Symbols, gifts, or tokens cannot maintain a loving relationship, nor can they be nurtured by some never-received expectations of vocalized love or forgiveness. Relationships must be nurtured and strengthened constantly with words of love and encouragement. If you do not express your positive, loving, and caring thoughts through kindness, your relationships will surely vanish. Don't let another opportunity slip away. Tell someone today how much you care. Give it a try!

Thoughts to Ponder

- You love yourself notwithstanding your faults, and you ought to love your friends in the same manner.
- Did you know the best way to be successful is to follow the advice you give others?
- Be careful that your marriage doesn't become a duel instead of a duet.
- Three things in life that may never be lost are love, hope, and honesty.

"To love your neighbor as you love yourself is not just a moral mandate. It's a psychological mandate."
—*James Lynch*

You were created to be loved and to love in return. But in order to love your neighbors, you must first love yourself. And since you are only able to give what you have and teach what you know, you must learn a little about self-love. First, it is impossible to love others more than you love yourself. Second, love is a limitless resource, and that means your opportunities to share that love are also limitless. Third, being kind to others will result in a healthier, happier you. And finally, realizing being with people you love and who love you is most important. Loving oneself is not a leisure time activity, but rather it is really hard work. So starting now your goal should be to develop the best possible self you can with the ability to share your love with others. Always remember that your God loves you, so how can you not love yourself?

Thoughts to Ponder

- Why is it that some people are so busy adding up their troubles that they forget about counting their blessings?
- Be brave. Even if you're not, pretend to be. No one can tell the difference.
- Avoid sarcastic remarks and never deprive someone of hope. It might be all they have.
- It isn't your position that allows you to love and to be loved; it's your disposition.

"We suffer from seeing to much death and not enough life, too much sorrow and not enough joy, too much greed and not enough giving, too much loneliness and not enough love."
—Unknown

With mass communication (TV, radio, and the Internet) our lives are so inundated and overrun by hate, greed, violence, and selfishness that we sometimes overlook the fact that there is at least an equal amount of goodness in the world. The problem is that those who promote their negativity and hate seem to be far more vocal than the silent majority. The lovers and positive thinkers of the world are certainly not given equal media time. You need to enjoy your blessings, be more giving, more loving, and be a person who just plain celebrates life daily. There has never been a more important time than now for you to get vocal and publicize goodness and display care and love. You cannot win if you do not begin!

Thoughts to Ponder

- How long did it take to learn that your words are the windows to your heart? Or have you?
- The only fool bigger than the person who knows it all is the person who argues with him.
- Forgive your enemies. It messes with their heads.
- People don't care how much you know until they know how much you care.

"Everyday is a happy day. Some days are just happier than others."

—*Donny Murphy*

How do you make today the best it can be? When encountering rough interactions with others, instead of analyzing and blaming them, re-evaluate your own feelings and needs. You can't force people to change their attitude, so focus on and adjust yours. The best defense is a good offense, so try spending more time with people who delight in being with you and you with them. Choose to be around people who are outgoing, open to change, loving, and happy, and choose to do things in life that you love doing. Choose those things that create in you a joyous and friendly attitude, such as reading, golfing, going to movies, writing, or maybe taking a trip. Make today a happy day and share with others what you have learned about yourself, your spouse, your children, and your pets. When you choose positive behavioral responses to situations with an upbeat attitude, you are helping to create your own happiness.

Thoughts to Ponder

- Isn't it nice to know all people smile in the same language?
- To be happy at home is the ultimate aim of all ambition.
- The foolish man seeks happiness in the distance; the wise man grows it under his feet.
- *There is no psychiatrist in the world like a puppy licking your face.*

"Happiness is inward and not outward, so it does not depend on what we have, but on what we are."
—*Henry Van Dyke*

Some people are convinced they are measured by their possessions, and that those possessions will bring them happiness. It seems the more you obtain in life, the more you want. After you buy, you are continually induced to discard and buy newer and better and more. Faster cars, bigger homes, louder alarms, and more insurance all fit the docket and, just as computers, they are outdated or out of fashion within hours of their purchase. It's easy to forget that living and loving are two of your most valuable possessions and they do not depreciate. Unfortunately, you only become aware of their value when you are faced with their loss. Becoming thankful for them is a lesson you sometimes fail to learn until it is too late, and, as you know, life goes by faster as you get older. Slow down and work on your inward happiness by sharing an act of kindness with someone who's having a hard time.

Thoughts to Ponder

- The best time to make friends is before you need them.
- Did you know that friendship is similar to sound health? The value is seldom known until it is lost.
- You cannot live a perfect day, even though you earned your money, unless you have done something for someone who will never be able to repay you.
- Having children makes you no more of a parent than having a piano makes you a pianist.

"The movement from certainty to uncertainty is sometimes called fear. Most of us want to have our minds continually occupied so that we are prevented from facing our fears."

—*Unknown*

Certainty without fear in life is something all of us want at one time or another. Unfortunately for us, the Lord made uncertainty a simple thing in the world, making certainty much more complicated and harder to achieve. He gives us just enough variation (uncertainty) in life to keep life from being boring, yet we continually look for sureness. Uncertainty makes life exciting, challenging, and interesting by not knowing what's around the corner or what will happen next. Assurance can develop into huge liabilities, such as giving you or lulling you into a false sense of security. This false security lowers your ability to make decisions based on the past and in many cases keeps you from preparing for the future. Here's to hoping you can understand the gift of uncertainty, learn from it, delight in it, and most of all use it to lower your fear factor.

Thoughts to Ponder

- That right person cannot and will not make your life complete. Once you have accepted that fact, you will be eligible for a happy, fulfilling relationship.
- The world gives itself to us. It gives itself freely to us and showers us with gifts, if we just allow it.
- Reasoning with a child is fine if you can reach the child's reason without destroying your own.
- Out of the mouths of babes come words you shouldn't have said in the first place.

"Far away in the sunshine are my highest inspirations. I may not reach them, but I can look up and see the beauty, believe in them, and try to follow where they lead."
—*Louisa May Alcott*

When pursuing your dreams, try not to lose sight of your God-given blessings of happiness, joy, love, and contentment. It can happen, especially when your focus is upon physical possessions. Throughout life we are given everything in proportion to our needs, but we still have a tendency to put a premium on things that are not abundant, such as diamonds, baseball cards, or things that are not really needed for true happiness. Earth was made for us to explore, to learn, to love, to play, and to enjoy life on, not to dominate over or to accumulate an inordinate amount of anything. Once you realize this you will find yourself enjoying life more, being happier, and being pleased with your non-physical blessings such as happiness, joy, and contentment. So reach for your dreams, believe in and follow them, see the beauty in them, but never forget to put a premium on the abundant blessings and free things of life. And life itself will be your sunshine.

Thoughts to Ponder

- Things that happen or are achieved by you were born in your imagination and dreams.
- Don't you love to try new things when people say you can't do them?
- Your child's love for you makes them want to adopt your best traits and learn the qualities that you urge upon them.
- If God is your copilot, swap seats!

"Inside myself is a place where I live alone, and that's where I renew my springs that never dry up."

—*Pearl S. Buck*

Some people comment that I always seem to be myself. Usually I tell them, "For years I tried to be somebody else and it didn't work." Trying to be what you are not is frustrating. It is full of worries, anxiety, and false expectations. To become who you are and to be treated as who and what you are, you must first know the real you. A career is developed in public; however, the real you is born and matured in your soul and inner spirit. Draw on your eternal springs by renewing your spiritual bonds with meditation. The strengthening of your faith will allow you to visit your inner thoughts and restore your self-image and confidence. The real you can be found not by trying to be what you are not, but in just being who you are. As you continue to renew your self-love and confidence, you get an extra special blessing, that of enriched interpersonal relationships.

Thoughts to Ponder

- When you fail, it's usually because you took the path of least persistence.
- Life is a compromise of what your ego wants to do, what experience tells you to do, and what your nerves let you do.
- It doesn't hurt to be optimistic. You can always cry later.
- At work, I sometimes wonder if change is impossible, except from the vending machines.

"Half of the unhappiness in the world is due to the failure of plans that were never reasonable and often impossible."
—*Edgar Watson Howe*

Do your plans involve travel, or to be successful at work or in romance? The secret to avoiding unhappiness is to not have unreasonable expectations and to make the appropriate preparations ahead of time. Becoming president of your company or traveling around the world this year may be unreasonable expectations, but a promotion or a trip to the Old Country to trace your family tree may be much more attainable. In planning, did you consider the requirements for that new position at work, your education, and competition? For the trip, what about your large house payment, the new car you need, furniture, or the fact that you haven't saved much money lately? If you want to advance and be successful, you had better start planning how to get there and begin preparations now. It would be nice to accomplish your goals without a whole lot of effort, but you and I know that will not happen. Successes that provides lasting values does not happen without preparation, planning, and, in some cases, conflict.

Thoughts to Ponder

- Skill is fine, and genius splendid, but at times the right personal contacts are more valuable.
- The most important ingredient in success is to know how to get along with people.
- Man's reach should exceed his grasp, or what's a heaven for?
- Billy Graham once said, "The only time my prayers are never answered is when I'm playing golf."

> "The happy man is the man who, without any direct search for happiness, inevitably finds joy in the act of giving, loving, and forging ahead and attaining the fullness and finality of his own self."
> —Pierre Teilhard De Chardin

At home and work you will encounter disappointments and setbacks, but they are not reason enough to stop reaching for success and happiness. Be careful not to fall victim to the idea that your happiness is not attainable, you are jinxed, and/or the world is against you. At any given time, you may lose your love or even your job, but neither is cause for long-term unhappiness. Don't lose heart; you are fine as long as you have hope, and remember that when one door closes another door opens. Happiness is an imaginary condition that the living often say the dead have attained. Adults often say that children are the happy ones, while some children say that adults are the happy ones. Isn't it interesting that the moment you are conscious of your happiness, you want more and for some reason you are no longer happy?

Thoughts to Ponder

- You should make the most of all that comes your way and the least of all that goes.
- Why is it that worry often gives a small thing a big shadow?
- You have the ability to see what no one else sees, so listen when others talk and stay optimistic when others are pessimistic.
- I've decided that working out is not for me. My new philosophy is now no pain, no pain.

"It takes the same amount of courage to have tried and failed as it does to have tried and succeeded."
—*Anne Morrow Lindbergh*

Remember your New Year's resolutions? Even if you didn't accomplish any of them, you obviously wanted to improve yourself or change directions in some way. Don't wait for the New Year to change something in your life or set new goals. Start now with small tasks, little goals, or simple objectives, and as you complete one, add another new one to your list. Set positive and realistic goals; write them on paper so you can refer to them regularly. Guess what? If you do this, you are more likely to stay focused to achieve them. Some examples would be to learn a new skill, commit to being more positive and appreciative, make better use of your time, plan a vacation, lower your debt, and save some money. You could spend more time with your family, pursue a hobby, plan your retirement, get your last will and testament completed, lose weight, or start an exercise plan. Have courage and stay persistent.

Thoughts to Ponder

- Set goals, but remember, achieving them will not be accidental but must certainly be worked at.
- Did you know more tears are shed over answered prayers than unanswered ones?
- You don't have to get all of it right all of the time.
- If quitters never win, and winners never quit, what fool came up with "Quit while you're ahead"?

"We can do whatever we wish to do, provided our positive thinking is strong enough. What do you most want to do? That's what you have to keep asking yourself in the face of difficulties."

—Katherine Mansfield

When having difficulties at home, with your friends, or going through a change in work status, it is very important that you never let yesterday's disappointments use up today's attitude. With each door that closes, another opens, and the width of the opening depends on your attitude. Try starting each day with an attitude adjustment or a ritual of thankfulness for what you have. Thank your Lord for blessings of life, family, job, friends, home, and for being alive. Beginning on a positive note will help in keeping you focused and remind you that life comes bearing its own special gifts. So untie the ribbon, review your God-given gifts and blessings, be grateful, be happy, and then do what you have to do: move on. And remember to always see your glass as half-full!

Thoughts to Ponder

- Isn't it great to know that if you exude happiness, it makes you a magnet, drawing others to you?
- When wronged, strike a balance between forgiving and forgetting.
- If you have changes going on in your life, thankfulness will allow you to keep an upbeat attitude.
- If you are going to throw a golf club, it is important to throw it ahead of you, down the fairway, so you don't have to waste energy going back to pick it up.

"Love doesn't just sit there like a stone. It has to be made, like bread—remade all the time, made new."
—*Ursula K. Leguin*

I know you have heard of physical abuse and verbal abuse. But have you heard of verbal neglect or of unsaid expectations? Verbally giving and sharing should be of primary concern in love relationships instead of just gifts that do not really say how much someone means to you. Symbols and tokens will not maintain or fully develop a lasting relationship. If you have warm, loving feelings, express them; don't assume he or she knows how you feel. Love has a tough time surviving, let alone surviving under continued verbal neglect. When left to sit there all alone, it will eventually wither and die. Don't wait for the announcement that your spouse or close friend wants out of the relationship to change your ways. Your relationships need to be nurtured and strengthened, or they will surely not grow and may vanish.

Thoughts to Ponder

- Remember that for every flower that has ever bloomed, it had to go through a whole lot of dirt to get there.

- Shared grief is half the sorrow, but happiness, when shared, is doubled.

- Bring into your relationship what you have to give and share, and then communicate and make it work.

- Remember your vows, promises, and commitments to one another. Honor what you've said to one another always and when you do drop the ball (because everyone makes mistakes), be the bigger person and don't avoid it. Talk about it and discuss how to get back on track again.

-

"Was it always in my nature to remember bad times and block out the good times or to think that success was an accident and failure seemed the only truth?"
—Lillian Hellman

Talk about a negative outlook on life. It's been a long time since I've had that attitude, how about you? Your approach to life should be to keep the good times alive, learn from but bury the bad experiences, and look forward to success and happiness. Blocking out the negative allows you to believe that life is worth living. You can and will produce great results when you are thoroughly sincere in incorporating the concept of positive thinking in your life. If you feel yourself leaning to the negative side, try to keep focused on the positive. Like working out at the gym, you must keep doing it one more time until you get it right. With stick-to-itiveness, you will see yourself going from the attitude of *I think I can* to that of *I know I can.*

Thoughts to Ponder

- Dwelling on "I should have" solves nothing. It's the next thing that will happen that needs to be thought about.
- Life is a long line of opportunities: They multiply when seized on, but die when neglected.
- To learn a new habit is important because it will help you gain the substance of life.
- It is almost impossible to remember how tragic a place the world is when one is playing golf.

> "Luck is not chance, it's toil; fortune's expensive smile is earned."
>
> —*Emily Dickinson*

Life is never absent of problems, yet some people fall apart at the first little thing that happens to them. Others accept those problems as opportunities to learn and to grow from and as such they are seen as having all the luck. But being lucky is not all that it appears, and in most cases being lucky takes confrontation, endurance, and the persistence to face obstacles with a positive attitude and then move on. Each obstacle should be viewed as a stone on which you can sharpen your knife. Learn to accept the unacceptable, do without the indispensable, and bear the unbearable. Remember, good luck and fortune are not cheap, they have to be earned.

Thoughts to Ponder

- You can grow only as much as your horizon allows.
- Remember, no matter how much you can do, no matter how engaging your personality may be, success involves working with and through others.
- Those who don't know that failure is inevitable achieve success.
- It only takes a second to open wounds in the people you love, yet it takes many years to heal them.

"With all your heart, love them enough to discipline them before it is too late, and when they have a tantrum, don't have one of your own."

—*Unknown*

This thought could be from the TV series *The Nanny*. When you teach your children not to have tantrums, do you learn from the lesson yourself? Each time you teach them to make social adjustments and you see positive results, it not only helps build their self-esteem but your parental ego also gets a boost. As a parent, the most important examples to show them are confidence and self-assurance. It's important to keep your composure by not having your own tantrum during and after confrontations. Remember, children are natural mimics, imitating your words and deeds. Having a grateful attitude for all you have rather than griping about what you don't have will help your children to maintain a good perspective of life. If you lose something—your job, your loved ones, or your health—take time to reflect on and be thankful for what you have. Try not to fly off the handle with your loved ones, and don't put yourself in a position of regret for what you say or do in that moment of anger.

Thoughts to Ponder

- Don't let anger heat up the fire in your soul, as you may singe yourself.
- If you have good sense to be slow to anger, then it is to your honor to overlook an offense.
- True love is when someone hurts you and you get so mad you don't yell because you know it would hurt his or her feelings.
- The most valuable thing in life is not what you have in it but whom you have in it.

"We often, almost sulkily, reject the good that God offers us because, at the moment, we expected some other good."
-C. S. Lewis

This quote reminds me of the Garth Brooks song "Unanswered Prayers." Had the man's prayers been answered originally, he would have never met the love of his life many years later, who became his wife. Expectations of your prayers yet unanswered can create blinders to the true blessings of your life. Not getting your desired wants could let you miss the beauty of your actual life while you're lusting after a mythical perfect one. When a prayer is not answered the way you want or when you want, maybe it has been answered, just not the way you wanted. You may not recognize it for days, weeks, or even years, but it will be answered, so don't waste your time living in a dream world of expectations. You choose how you respond to what is happening; it's your choice, so make it wisely.

Thoughts to Ponder

- Your greatest glory is not in never failing, but in rising up every time you fail.

- Your commitment helps you look toward a future that cannot be seen yet promises to be there.

- Believe it or not, friendships can help you ward off depression, boost your immune systems, lower your cholesterol levels, increase your odds of surviving coronary disease, and keep stress hormones in check.

- Coincidence is when God chooses to remain anonymous.

"The more light you allow within you, the brighter the world you live in will be."

—*Shakti Gawain*

When life deals you a bad hand, can you let it go, learn from the experience, and focus on more positive things? Although there are plenty of things in life to be annoyed at, angered with, or hurt by, it doesn't mean you should ignore all that is beautiful, good, and lights up your life in positive ways. Look for the hidden blessings of difficult situations. When things are going well and you are happy, try not to think of times in your life when there was a crisis or tragedy. Say to yourself, *If that had not happened in my life, I wouldn't be here at this time and place, enjoying and loving my life as it is now. It may have been difficult at the time of that crisis, but now I am happy and can move on. It's my responsibility to learn from it, to brighten up my life, and to create joy for myself.* When you project happiness and you are smiling, the whole world smiles with you.

Thoughts to Ponder

- A time will come when you will realize that you haven't only been specializing in something, but that something has been specializing in you.
- Depression is merely anger without enthusiasm.
- Be thankful for the shadow that watches your work because it means that you're out in the sunshine.
- A truly happy person is one who can enjoy the scenery on a detour.

"The value of life lies not in the length of your days, but in the use you make of them. Satisfaction and happiness in life depend not on the number of your days, but on your will, your attitude, and how you focus on daily events."
—*Michel de Montaigne*

Your persistence to focus on positive thoughts will add value to each and every day. Expressing your gratitude daily can enhance the value of your life and the many blessings it holds. The more aware you become of things for which you are thankful, the easier it becomes to express your thankfulness. And it seems the more persistent you are about giving thanks, the more you have for which to be thankful. Conversely, when you are unaware of your blessings and show little appreciation for them by being ungrateful, the more things around you tend to look bleak, dismal, or fall apart. Persistent daily focus on attitude is kind of like an insurance policy to help assure good things continue to come your way. In reality, when you focus on the abundance in your life, your life feels abundant. So fill each day with satisfaction by focusing on your blessings.

Thoughts to Ponder

- It's eerie to learn that the one who fears what one may suffer already suffers what they fear.
- The Grand Canyon proves that even mountains are no match for the power of persistence.
- All will be judged individually on his own merits and not as a group on a comparison basis. So don't compare yourself to others.
- I'm thankful for my puppy that licks my face even after I left him alone all day.

"It's pretty hard to tell what does bring happiness when poverty and wealth have both failed."
—*Kin Hubbard*

Neither wealth nor splendor is a sure thing for bringing you the happiness you desire, so don't confuse wealth and success with happiness. In reality, tranquility at home and success at work are better bets for leading to happiness. The best bet is sharing your love with others. It may just be one of the greatest gifts you have to give to make yourself and others happy. Making others happy is a sure way of bringing you that tranquility you have been looking for. First Corinthians 13:2 says, "If I have a faith that can move mountains, but have not love, I am nothing." Verse 13 says, "And now these three remain: faith, hope, and love. But the greatest of these is love." So share your love, don't deprive others of it, and remember, when you give of yourself, you are freed from your own self-absorption. The end result is the more you give, the happier you will be.

Thoughts to Ponder

- Talk is cheap because supply exceeds demand.
- Love is when you tell someone some bad news about yourself and fear they won't love you anymore and you get surprised because not only do they still love you, they love you even more.
- When you share love and feel good about yourself, you cannot be threatened by the future.
- Love is when you go out to eat and give somebody most of your freedom fries without asking him or her for any.

> "I have learned, in whatsoever state I am in, to be content."
>
> —St. Paul

Each of us has three major circles of influence: you, other people, and life itself. You influence and are influenced by others just as life influences you and is influenced by you. The question is whether you are willing to embrace what shows up in your life in a positive way and make adjustments instead of self-indulging yourself in pity? Unless you openly accept and embrace your circumstances, you will never get the benefits of the lessons life is trying to teach you. Being grateful for what happens can make the experience bearable and lead you to contentment. It is acceptance and contentment with what happens that will make you happy in the moment. In the weeks to come, whenever you encounter something that is not comfortable and does not make you happy, ask yourself, *How is this right for me, and what function or need is this event serving?* Keep a mental record so that the lessons won't have to be learned again, and remember, the happiness you project will have a positive influence on those around you.

Thoughts to Ponder

- Look for the hidden blessings of difficult situations.
- The best things you can give your children, next to good habits, are good memories.
- Life is the soul's nursery, and it is the training place for your destiny into eternity.
- "The Lord bless you and keep you; the Lord make His face shine upon you, and be gracious to you; the Lord lift up His countenance upon you, and give you peace." (Numbers 6:24–26)

> *"Think positively and masterfully, with confidence and faith, and life becomes more secure, active, and richer in achievement and experience."*
>
> —*Eddy Rickenbacker*

In all of your relationships, be as positive and upbeat as you can be and your life will take on a new zest, deeper interest, and a greater meaning. When you are upbeat and positive, you are bound to become an excited person full of life. In addition, your attitude will become infectious, building inspiration, excitement, and joy to those around you. Your life will be richer, fuller, more exciting, more secure, and you will be able to have lasting enjoyment. Only the wisest can achieve lasting enjoyment, and that can only be done when you have confidence, faith, and an optimistic attitude. The optimistic outlook is the key path that leads to that achievement and happiness. Each day is the beginning of a new life, so seize it, live it, and enjoy it.

Thoughts to Ponder

- If your ship doesn't come in, swim out to it.
- No matter how big or soft or warm your bed is, you still have to get out of it.
- If you borrow money, you should borrow it from a pessimist, as he or she doesn't expect it back.
- If you begin with certainties, there is a chance you can end up in doubt; but if you are content to begin with doubts, there is a good chance you will end up with certainties.

"Life is like a blanket that is too short. When you pull it up, your toes rebel, and when you yank it down, you shiver and your shoulders get cold. Cheerful folks manage to draw their knees up and have a very comfortable night."

—*Marion Howard*

One way to make your marriage successful and comfortable is to remember it is more than just the wedding vows and the passionate embraces. When you feel the blanket of life is too short, draw in your knees, and remember, a loving relationship is also three meals a day, sharing the workload, and remembering to carry out the trash. Being totally comfortable under your blanket of life is when you know that your best friend and soul mate can do anything or do nothing and you will still have a great time together. If you follow God's rules for marriage, all husbands will feel respected and each wife will feel loved.

Thoughts to Ponder

- Happiness is a sunset; it is there for all, but many of us look the other way and lose it.
- When seeking contentment, expect troubles as being inevitable. So try repeating to yourself these comforting words: This too shall pass.
- It's eerie that what worries you masters you!
- Many people are hurt and angered when their mates try to change them. Realize that the only person that you can change is yourself. Leave the changing in God's hands and pray for God's intersession in the marriage.

"Creating success is tough. But keeping it is tougher. You have to keep producing, you can never stop."

—*Pete Rose*

Life can be really rough at times with its many problems and with your many errors in judgment. You can choose to learn from your mistakes and move on, or you can remain stagnant by repeating them over and over. It's time for a little faith and hope in your pursuit, but keep in mind that faith and hope are just two of the risks that *must* be taken in life to achieve success. Decide what it is you want to accomplish, make detailed plans to get there, and then just do it. That's pretty straightforward and easy to say, but at times it is hard to stay focused. A friend sent me the following daily reminder on how to succeed:

"The road to success is not straight; you will encounter a curve called failure, a loop called confusion, speed bumps called friends, red lights called enemies, and caution lights called family. You will have flats along the way called jobs but if you have a spare called determination, an engine called perseverance, insurance called faith, and a driver called God, you will make it to a place called success."

Thoughts to Ponder

- Don't be afraid to make a mistake. Go ahead and goof.
- Making the simple complicated is commonplace; making the complicated simple, that's creativity.
- Try to remember that if the Lord brings you to it, He will get you through it.
- I've often thought that if I had my life to live over, I'd make the same mistakes, only sooner.

> *"You can work at something for twenty years and come away with twenty years' worth of valuable experience, or you can come away with one year's experience twenty times."*
>
> —*Gwen Jackson*

I think you will agree that falling in love is easy. Keeping the romance, excitement, and love alive year after year is the challenge. The first years are usually easy, and then we are confronted with how to make the next year and the next different, exciting, challenging, and as enjoyable as the first. The key is the learning experiences gained from the early years and how you put them to use. If you don't adapt and stay with the "same ole, same ole" stuff year after year, you end up with one year's worth of experience after twenty years. A balance is needed between the traditional serious approaches to romance and the lighter and brighter side of romance. To maintain your sanity, the magnificent author Leo Buscaglia says you need love, laughter, and romance in your relationships. So laugh and play on your journey of love. And remember, your mind, spirit, and intellect require continual attention and stimulation in the world of love. What better way to stimulate them than with play and laughter?

Thoughts to Ponder

- Living involves tearing up one rough draft after another.
- If you take a good look around, you'll find real life is funny!
- Always keep your words soft and sweet, just in case you have to eat them.
- Did you know the best angle to approach any problem from is the try-angle?

"A loving touch makes the difference."
—*Unknown*

Did you know affection and non-sexual touching are tremendous resources for both physical and emotional being? Both are also essential to your personal and professional growth as well. Think about it: without your mom and dad's or family members' love, or Grandma and Grandpa's affection, the loving touch of your spouse, hugs at your church, or the care, concern, and encouraging caress of healthcare professionals in the hospital, we might as well live like animals. To give and receive these loving actions is free and anyone can do it. You need no special equipment, and the supply is always abundantly available. To love we must let people know we care, and the best way is to literally reach out and show them as often as possible. Show someone the physical and emotional touches of love. Make their day! And yours!

Thoughts to Ponder

- Did you know the strength of a person isn't in the width of their shoulders—it is seen in the width of their arms that circle you?
- The strength of a person isn't in how hard they hit. It's in how tender they touch.
- Have a firm handshake, look people in the eye, and say thank you often!
- Getting or giving one hug each day is the best show of appreciation ever. Give that hug, get that hug, you will be rewarded with a heart full of joy.

"You cannot belong to anyone else until you belong to yourself."

—*Pearl Bailey*

Your self-respect is the companion of your self-worth. The judgments you pass on yourself are reflected in your every decision and act. Keep in mind, the less you think of yourself, the poorer your decisions will be. When you have a poor self-worth, the odds are that others will treat you like a doormat. Be positive about your self-worth and keep this in mind: You are just as wise, intelligent, interesting, and desirable as others. So concentrate on your strengths, talents, and self-esteem, because no one will think you are a worthy individual until you do. Be persistent about your importance and worthiness and don't take guilt trips. Instead take a trip to the mall, to the next county, to a foreign country, but *not* to where the guilt is.

Thoughts to Ponder

- Ask yourself, *Is it better to be silent and considered a fool, or should I speak and remove all doubt?*
- Tell your spouse that if he or she lives to be a hundred, you want to live to be a hundred minus one day, so you never have to live without them.
- Let's be thankful for the fools. If it weren't for them, the rest of us could not succeed.
- When you are feeling depressed, think of the woman in dire straits, working twelve hours a day, seven days a week, trying to feed her children.

"Trust your hunches. They're usually based on facts filed away just below the conscious level."
—Dr. Joyce Brothers

With a crisis looming in your life, what should you do? When you stand at that fork in the road, which way do you turn? You can focus on the negative side of a problem and feel victimized, or you can look at a problem as an opportunity for a new beginning. If you genuinely do not love what you do and you are going to be unhappy, what good is it to have success? Are you sure the promotion, that prestigious position, or new lifestyle is worth it? When you need help, your God answers knee-mail, and making decisions with a little help from your inner soul never hurts. Your faith will help you sort out those facts filed away below your conscious level and help get you where you should be. So start now; make decisions by opening your heart to the lessons of life you have learned. "Trust your hunches" or your "gut reactions"; it may well be the Spirit within you talking.

Thoughts to Ponder

- Did you know that each hunch you have is creativity trying to tell you something?
- When you decide something with kindness, you will usually make the right decision.
- Fall in love with yourself and you have no rivals.
- Have trust, and when nothing makes sense and you are confused or frustrated, remember: God has a solution.

"You don't just luck into things. You build step by step, whether it's friendships or opportunities."
—*Barbara Bush*

People need each other, and you cannot succeed alone. Knowing how to plan and work with others toward achieving goals will provide you with strength through cooperation. Acknowledging those who encourage you and help you is a way of sharing success. The planning, scheduling, persistence, working hard, and setting goals and timetables have nothing to do with luck. If no one is with you to celebrate when you become successful, what good is it anyway? Remember how you got there and who really helped you succeed and that friends are those who reach for your hand and touch your heart.

Thoughts to Ponder

- Have you ever heard that opportunity doesn't knock, it just whispers, and that luck is a by-product of busting your fanny?
- Humility is only gratitude.
- When success comes your way, keep in mind that knowledge is horizontal, and wisdom is vertical and comes down from above.
- The day is yours. Don't throw it away. Since you woke up breathing, congratulations! You have another chance!

"It is possible to be different and still be all right."
—*Ann Wilson Schaef*

Every person adds to his or her recipe of life a unique personality with varied temperaments and styles. Your personal temperaments, styles, and attitudes are your gifts to the recipe making up the menu of life. Just as the seasonings of a fine meal with herbs and flavoring are different for each meal, each of us brings something different that makes our life unique. These differences in human behavior and those of other individuals are what make life fascinating, a challenge, and so very interesting. Try to keep in mind that it is acceptable to be different and the more of these differences you can understand and accept, the more fulfilled and loving your life will become. The French say, *"Vive la difference,"* which means, "Live with your differences." Always be true to your feelings and dare to be different; you'll be all right!

Thoughts to Ponder

- Keep an eraser nearby to remind you that everyone makes mistakes, and it's okay.
- Is it not awesome to know that sharing your knowledge is a way to achieve mortality?
- Open your arms to change, but don't let go of your values.
- The Buddhists say, "You can explore the universe looking for somebody who is more deserving of your love and affection than you are yourself, and you will not find that person anywhere."

"Never lose sight of the fact that the most important yardstick of your success will be how you treat other people—your family, friends, coworkers, and even strangers you meet along the way."

—*Barbara Bush*

Everyone gossips. You cannot help but gossip in one form or fashion, especially with close friends. And how you talk about, treat, and act toward others is a reflection of who you really are. Did you know as much good can be done by good gossip as harm by bad gossip? So if you are going to talk about others, why don't you be what I would call a "Golden Gossip"? Someone once told me that he had a friend who always talked about his friends and neighbors but made it his business to talk of them without ever saying anything but good. Yes, he was a gossip, but he was "Golden Gossip." Be careful what you say; the tongue can be a powerful weapon for good or evil, and remember to always treat others as you would like to be treated. "If you can't say something nice, don't say anything at all" should be your golden rule.

Thoughts to Ponder

- Keep skunks and gossips at a distance.
- No matter how good friends may be, they're going to hurt you every once in a while, and you must forgive them for that.
- There are four things you can't recover: the stone after it's thrown, the word after it's said, the occasion after it's lost, and time after it's passed.
- Here's a rumor to pass around: The only two tools you need are WD-40 and duct tape. If it doesn't move and it should, use WD-40. If it moves and shouldn't, use the tape.

> *"We cannot tell the precise moment when friendship is formed. As in filling a vessel drop by drop, there is at last a drop which makes it run over."*
>
> *—James Boswell*

Each time you meet someone new, there is the potential for a new friendship, and that new and true friend can be a wonderful part of your world. You can never have enough friends, and to have your cup run over with friendship would be wonderful. When you find companions with whom you have things in common, who enjoy good conversation with positive attitudes, it is wise to apply the "oil of politeness" treatment to the mechanism of developing friendship. If they have faith and believe and are hopeful that the many problems of the world are fixable, then that's a plus in developing grounds for those friendships. Once you find your new best friend, the foremost thing you can do is to be their friend.

Thoughts to Ponder

- Medicine for your many enemies is one friend.
- A day without sunshine is like, well, night.
- Isn't it amazing to know creativity may become addictive, and when it does, you cannot live without it?
- Each day is for toil, and some hours are for sport, but for friends, life is too short.

"When you don't have any money, the problem is food. When you have money, it's sex. When you have both, you have a health problem. If everything is simply "Jake," then you're frightened of death."

—*J.P. Donleavy*

Along life's bumpy road we all know it is important to face our problems head on. We are supposed to draw from our past solutions and lessons learned and apply them to the new problematic situation. And on it goes; with each problem solved, along comes another. Since you now have lots of experience to draw from, why not consider each new one as a challenge and rise to the occasion and ask, "What can I learn from this situation?" The keys to mastering this technique are avoiding the fear of failure and being steadfast to perseverance. Success breeds success, so with each resolution of a problem you will get a feeling of achievement, fulfillment, and happiness, as well as a reservoir to draw from in the future. With a few successions and a little faith, your worries will subside, and when everything is "simply Jake," death and taxes will be easier to accept.

Thoughts to Ponder

- God gave us burdens, and he also gave us shoulders.
- Conflict builds character. Crisis defines it.
- Whether you're a writer, homemaker, athlete, musician, plumber, administrative assistant, businessman, or retiree, there is no way around it! When you work hard at it, you'll win; if you don't, you won't.
- Did you know everyone has a photographic memory? It's just that some don't have film?

"I can't tell anybody what to do, and I try not to give advice. Instead, I say, "This is what we know about this problem at this time, and here are the consequences of these actions."

—Dr. Joyce Brothers

Advice is what you ask for when you already know the answer. The day you stop making excuses and take complete responsibility for yourself is the day you start moving on with your life. This is true in your personal as well as your business life. Being accountable and not blaming others when you goof allows you to take responsibility for those actions and gives you the power to change those things. Turn your thoughts and conversations around to be positive and power-packed with faith, hope, love, and action; that is when mistakes will fail in their mission. The consequence of not accepting accountability for your actions allows you to give up your power to change things for yourself and others.

Thoughts to Ponder

- When you are experiencing or having a self-pity party, remember, shopping is cheaper than a psychiatrist is.
- When you lose money, you lose a lot, and when you lose a friend, you lose much more, but when you lose your faith, you lose all.
- Marriage is a work in progress, so keep working on it.
- Have you ever wondered how there can be self-help *groups?*

"When you look for the good in others, you discover the best in yourself."

—*Martin Walsh*

When you are empathetic, you are aware of and attempt to understand the point of view, situation, feelings, and motives of others. It also means you are responsive to their situation and treat them as you would like to be treated. Practicing empathy in your personal and business relationships allows you to eliminate negative snap decisions or judgments. Step back for one moment and attempt to understand the other person's view by using the Ninety-Ten Principle. This means understanding "that only 10% of your life consists of what happened to you and 90% of your life is decided on how you reacted to what happened to you." If you are empathetic, you will be sensitive to the value of others' viewpoints even though your thinking is at odds with their opinion. And if you can develop empathy as a habit, you will no longer be ruled by the passion of the moment or preconceived opinions. You will have discovered the best in yourself, and your ability to love, to show gratitude, and to make sound decisions will become boundless.

Thoughts to Ponder

- When practicing empathy, ask yourself, *Do I want to experience peace of mind today, or do I want to experience conflict?*
- The roadblocks in life are only there for you to find a way around them.
- Did you know that if you want to be listened to, you should put in some time listening?
- Dilbert, in the cartoon series, says, "Tell me what you want and I'll tell you how to get along without it."

"Developing a servant's heart can be one of the most satisfying undertakings of your life. The more you learn to focus on blessing others, the more freely the blessings will flow in your life."

—*Thomas Kinkade*

When was the last time you befriended someone? At work, business, church, or social functions, your opportunities to do so are endless. Do you remember being in the position of being alone, not knowing anyone, or being the outsider? Wouldn't it have been nice if someone befriended you? Remember, everyone and everything is interconnected, and no wall is too high or strong enough to separate us from one another's loneliness or despair. Even if you convince yourself that you do not need other people, they need you. When you show kindness and concern for them, the blessings you will receive in return are enormous. Try sharing your blessings and love, as these are precious resources you can never run out of.

Thoughts to Ponder

- You don't have to change friends if you understand that friends change.
- Good friends are hard to find, harder to leave, and impossible to forget.
- Always be kind and thoughtful to others, for everyone you meet is fighting a hard battle in one way or another. Maybe harder than yours!
- It is not good to compare yourself to others. All will be judged individually on their own merits, not as a group on a comparison basis.

"Only in growth, reform, and change, paradoxically enough, is true security to be found."
—*Anne Morrow Lindbergh*

Life is unpredictable with its never-ending procession of unanticipated events such as reform, change, miracles, crises, blessings, and new opportunities. With all this unpredictability you can understand that it is absurd to think that you alone can control your life. Even if you believe there is a greater power in control, He has given you the freedom of choice, and it is your choices that will help you manage the way you respond to life's variables. As a work in progress, your daily decisions to adapt and to change will control your destiny. It's encouraging to know you can feel a little more secure when you make those decisions with optimism and positive thinking. The challenge is yours; you can go along for the rollercoaster ride, or you can find security in knowing you make the difference in the outcome of each day's events.

Thoughts to Ponder

- Never consent to cower when you have the impulse to soar.
- When making choices, don't have regrets; they are an appalling waste of energy. You can't build on them, and regrets are only good for wallowing in.
- Your life is like a jet plane: if it doesn't take off on time, keep working on the engines.
- Have you ever wondered, *Is it possible to be totally partial?*

"Life is no brief candle to me. It is a sort of splendid torch which I have got a hold of for the moment, and I want to make it burn as brightly as possible before handing it on to future generations."
—George Bernard Shaw

The incentive for living a life of love and fulfillment becomes extremely important when you realize that no one has forever. You are born and you die; seldom do you have a second chance for either. If you fear the future, you cannot enjoy the present, and if you deny mortality, you sometimes lack the driving force to face life enthusiastically. Without enthusiasm you lose sight of the significance of each moment and will tend to put them off for some future time. When you ignore those special moments of life, you lose them forever, and your candle of life will remain subdued. When you choose living over existing, enjoying life to the fullest and getting the most out of it by putting the most into it, your candle becomes a torch. Don't allow life to go by as a brief candle! Make yours more enjoyable now, and don't wait for your would-have, could-have, or should-have attitudes to become habitual.

Thoughts to Ponder

- Did you know time is your wisest counselor? Don't waste it worrying about the future.
- If you don't know where you are going, you will probably end up somewhere else.
- Rejoice in the way things are, and once you realize that nothing is missing, the whole world will belong to you.
- Every time someone comes to you complaining, accept their complaining or point out the positive side of life.

> "*Love has nothing to do with what you are expecting to get, only with what you are expecting to give, which is everything.*"
> —*Katharine Hepburn*

A miraculous energy flows between two people who care enough to get beyond the surface and games and truly share of themselves. When they reach that level of love, you can see it in their smile and that special glow that appears when two people have an outpouring of shared romantic experiences. It usually means they are willing to take the risks of being totally open, of listening, and of responding with their whole hearts. If you want to love and be loved and radiate that glow, you must be ready to give your all. True love is not shallow and thin love isn't love at all. Love is or it isn't and to be successful in love, you must be willing to reveal yourself to the one you love. Keep the romance alive by continually searching for new ways to enrich your relationship and remember your love is abundant—it comes from a never-ending source and that means you can never run out.

Thoughts to Ponder

- Follow your bliss. Find where it is and don't be afraid to follow it.
- If you give yourself as a wholehearted response to love, then love will wholeheartedly respond to you.
- No one is perfect. Your partner wants and deserves your willingness to understand and forgive them.
- Remember that no relationship can be sustained without forgiveness.

"Things do not change, we do."
—*Henry David Thoreau*

Unconditional love is something everyone yearns for. The problem is that it is hard to meet the condition of loving unconditionally. We are told that two people must come together as one and accept one another the way they are. That's how your relationship is supposed to be, without restrictions or conditions. In fact, for a successful relationship, just the opposite may be true. Only in growing separately can individuals grow together. When you encourage a change without conditions, you will find that your love for each other will begin to grow stronger. Your success will not be measured by your present circumstances, but rather by the obstacles you overcame in the growth process while reaching for happiness. It may be time to not only let your loved one grow, but maybe you should encourage it. Remember that any action that inhibits is not love. Love is only love when it liberates.

Thoughts to Ponder

- How long did it take to realize that you don't know what you've got until you lose it, and you won't know what you've been missing until it arrives?
- *A dog is the only thing on earth that loves you more than he loves himself.*
- When you start to make changes, every little bit helps and every little quit hurts.
- Unconditional love is when your puppy licks your face even after you left him alone all day.

"We have limitless control over what might be."
—*Unknown*

You, just as your friends and coworkers, are the product of your past experiences, fears, joys, triumphs, the people you have met, and your dreams. The important thing is not to be trapped or enslaved to your past. Attempting to live in the past is a sad alternative to living in the present. Start now by making a wonderful memory for tomorrow because everything you do now not only enriches your present, but also decides and enriches your future. You have limitless power and authority over what will be, so take control of your life. Let go of the past, get excited about the now, be positive, and make each day rewarding and joyous. In the country song "The Best Days" by George Strait the lyrics say, "Dad, this could be the best day of my life." I say *every* day is the best day of my life. How about you? What do you say?

Thoughts to Ponder

- You are like a stained glass window. You sparkle and shine when the sun is out, but when the darkness sets in, your true beauty will be revealed by the light from within.
- Take control of your life. Dare to dream and take risks. Compete!
- At times, using your imagination is more important than knowledge, but used together, wow!
- I like long walks, especially when people who annoy me take them.

"Be glad of life because it gives you the chance to love and to work and to play and to look up at the stars."
—*Henry Van Kyke*

You can accept setbacks that come to you in life with a sad acceptance, or you can rise up against them with all the human passion you can muster. Remember, "Life is yours to do with as you will." You can choose to find your life exciting or dull, full of bliss or sadness, or you can choose to fill it with ecstasy or emptiness. The point is that our Lord has given you the ability to make the choice. Your words, your dreams, and your thoughts have the power to create positive conditions in your life. What you speak about, you can bring about, and it is always better to choose the positives, especially when you consider the alternatives. Search for the stars, and don't be afraid to believe that you can have what you want and deserve.

Thoughts to Ponder

- Never underestimate your power to change yourself.
- Never overestimate your power to change others.
- Your happiest future will be based on your forgotten past since you can't move on in life until you let go of past failures and heartaches.
- If you treat your spouse like a thoroughbred they will never become a nag.

"Do not take for granted those people that are closest to your heart. Cling to them as you would your life, for without them, life is meaningless. It is a fragile thread that binds us to each other."

—*Unknown*

Do you know that thousands of children are being physically and verbally abused daily and elderly people are spending their final days without tenderness and love? You have the power to help and to heal people who are near and dear to you by merely outstretching a hand or by giving a warm hug. Nothing monumental is required, only simple things, such as making that phone call you have not made, sending that note you have put off writing, sharing a hug, or showing that kindness you have failed to show. The love you share is the fragile thread that binds you with your loved ones. The measure of a man is the gold on the inside, not the glitter on the outside. So make a stand by lending a hand to those you care for. When it comes to sharing your love, the opportunities you have are limitless.

Thoughts to Ponder

- A pat on the back helps build character if it's given often enough, hard enough, and long enough.
- Live so that when your children think of fairness, caring, and integrity, they think of you.
- Use your wit to amuse, not abuse.
- The best inheritance you can leave your children is a good example.

"It makes no difference how deeply seated may be the trouble, how hopeless the outlook, how muddled the tangle, how great the mistake. A sufficient realization of love will dissolve it all."
—*Emmit Fox*

Most of the things we worry about at home or at work almost never happen. I think we all know this from firsthand experience. Still, we hold on to our worry as if it would be frivolous to give it up. Worry makes fools of us all and tends to control our lives and leaves us with empty hearts and missed experiences. If only we could learn to love more and sort out real concerns from the imaginative and insignificant ones. For a realization of the spiritual gift of love, read 1 Corinthians 13 of your Bible. If your faith is wavering and you can't stop worrying, try reading Matthew 6:19–34, which talks about the treasures in Heaven and worry. It may help you to sort things out.

Thoughts to Ponder

- The highest pinnacle of the spiritual life is not joy in unbroken sunshine, but absolute and undoubting trust in the love of your Lord.
- Isn't it wonderful to know the more you invest in a marriage, the more valuable it becomes?
- If you love someone, put their name in a circle, instead of a heart, because hearts can break, but circles go on forever.
- When Grandmother got arthritis and couldn't bend over and paint her toenails, Grandpa started doing it for her all the time, even though his hands have arthritis. That's love.

> *"Do not dismiss your dreams. To be without dreams is to be without hope. To be without hope is to be without purpose."*
>
> —*Unknown*

Everyone has dreams, and everyone has the capacity to possess great hope. Your capacity for hope is significant in that it provides you with a sense of purpose and destination and gives you the energy to move forward in life. The point is that to reach those dreams requires hope. But hope must be accompanied with purpose, courage, and strength to be fulfilled. Once you realize that having hope is one of your greatest assets, you can begin to use it to your advantage. And remember, your hopes and dreams allow you to face the trials and tribulations of daily life. Keep in mind, there is no medicine like hope, no tonic more powerful than the belief that every problem has a solution. Never make fun of or laugh at those who don't have dreams of success. People who don't have dreams don't have much.

Thoughts to Ponder

- Did you know with hope you can change a potential tragedy into an achievement?
- If the situation won't change, then you should change to meet the situation.
- Let's hope you get all that you wish for and that all your dreams come true.
- Any problem we face can be handled, with God's help, one day at a time.

> *"It's not whether you get knocked down. It's whether you get up again."*
> —*Vincent Lombardi*

Wherever you are at work, home, or play, and you feel you're held back, pushed aside, ignored, hurt, or rejected, it is your reaction to the situation that counts. Do you quit trying or try the same approach again; do you try another less-aggressive path; or do you take control of the situation? Pull up your shirtsleeves; keep a positive attitude and try again. One of the most positive things you can do is to follow your own heart by continuing forward. The key is getting up, trying again, and, above all, you must be persistent. Keep in mind that there are very few obstacles that can resist your positive attitude, perseverance, determination, patience, and your love. If once you don't succeed, try and try again.

Thoughts to Ponder

- Don't be afraid of pressure because pressure is what turns a lump of coal into a diamond.
- Even a woodpecker owes his success to the fact that he uses his head.
- When will you learn that it's not your outlook but your up-look that counts?
- Man cannot discover new oceans unless he has the courage to lose sight of the shore.

"When you point a finger at someone else, remember that three of your fingers are pointing at yourself."
—*Unknown*

Some think that raising their voice or pointing an accusing finger is a way of asserting themselves. But guess what? You don't have to attack your friends, spouses, or coworkers to be assertive. In fact, effective assertiveness is most often demonstrated by being courteous, kind, and gentle. To be assertive in the positive sense, you should strive for a balance between standing up for what you believe to be right and what you know to be the rights of others. You must know what it is you want and how you feel about it, and then try to state these things simply, openly, and without anger or fear. If you catch yourself flying off the handle, make amends immediately because it's "easier to eat crow while it's still warm." Being tactful is still the simplest approach.

Thoughts to Ponder

- As long as you can, give the benefit of the doubt.
- Since God forgives you your past deeds, maybe you should imitate Him.
- Wasn't it great to learn sometimes you will regret opening your mouth, but you will rarely regret keeping it shut?
- Be courteous, kind, and gentle, and remember, "no" is a word that can never be misunderstood.

"Humor isn't for everyone. I believe it's only for people who want to have fun, enjoy life, and feel alive."
—*Anne Wilson Schaef*

When you fall in love, life takes on meaning and seems to have a purpose, and it seems like things could not get any better. The good news is, these new feelings of love, joy, and happiness can be enhanced with just a little sense of humor. Balance is necessary for happiness in all phases of your life, especially in love. The joy of being in love makes you more alive with each moment and brings with it unpredictability and a playful feeling that the world is a toy box. Balancing that love with unpredictability will allow you to laugh at the world and help keep your love alive. Those who have love combined with humor in their relationship will tell you that with this attitude it's not difficult to live on top of the mountain day after day. Don't worry; if you don't add humor to your love, nothing bad will happen to you, but you might just miss out on the joy of brightening up someone's day.

Thoughts to Ponder

- Did you know that you grow up the day you have your first real laugh at yourself?
- What you should do best is share your happiness and enthusiasm.
- The following is as true for life as it is for golf: "I hate golf, I hate golf, I hate golf. Nice shot. I love this game!"
- Have you ever wondered how it is that Tarzan never had a beard?

"The only true happiness comes from squandering ourselves for a purpose."
—*William Cooper*

Some people believe that at work and in their personal relationships they are emotionally safe when they remain guarded, unexposed, and thick-skinned. (Do you know anyone like this?) By trying not to reveal themselves to others, it gives them emotional security and protects them from any relationship other than a superficial one. In actuality, what it does is isolate a person into loneliness. Taking chances, moving outside of that comfort zone, and becoming vulnerable are the only ways you stand a chance of attaining true happiness. Someone once said, "Take a chance, work like you don't need the money, love like you've never been hurt, and dance like there is no one watching." Remember that vulnerability is the soul of love, and it is the stepping stone you must accept when seeking that elusive thing you call happiness.

Thoughts to Ponder

- When you become successful, it means that you have won the respect of intelligent people and the affection of children.
- Count your blessings, never overlooking the small ones, for a lot of small blessings add up to a big one.
- Step out of your comfort zone, but not in anger. It never brings good results to fly into a rage, and you almost always make bad landings.
- Isn't it enlightening to know life is an endless struggle full of frustrations and challenges, but eventually you will find a hairstylist or barber you like?

"There are none so blind as they who will not see."
—Unknown

A very large part of living, learning, communicating, and especially loving is done by the use of your senses, or "nonverbally." Learning to use the senses, especially sight, is a wonderful thing, and you will be, for the most part, freer and happier and more capable of loving because of it. Sight is one of the most precious gifts, and even when blessed with twenty-twenty vision and hindsight, few of us ever bother to use it to the fullest. People know what you are, and you know what they are, primarily by what you both see, not by what you both smell, touch, or hear. Never forget, when words deceive and eyesight fails, true love can be perceived fully through all of your senses. Even when you think your sight is perfect, don't be so blind as to not use all of your senses.

Thoughts to Ponder

- One thing you can learn by watching a clock is that it passes time by keeping its hands busy.
- Isn't it wonderful to know that swallowing angry words is much better than having to eat them?
- When someone is hugging you, let him or her be the first to let go.
- "We are all souls walking around in suits of skin."
  —Robert Zimmerman

"Whether or not interplanetary communications ever materialize, an even more grandiose project awaits us. This is the need for human beings to communicate with one another, here and now."

—*Norman Cousins*

Friendly acts or kind words can work magic for your relationships with others at home, work, or play. When sincerely given, these goodhearted expressions of kindness can work wonders. You can never become so above it all, so sophisticated, or so comfortable at your work or in a relationship that little gestures of kindness can be neglected. When asked, "How are you?" try saying, "Great!" instead of the basic, "Okay," or "Hanging in there." Not only will you feel and act better, so will others because your attitude is infectious. Don't limit or restrict your kindness. If expressions or gestures of kindness are good enough for total strangers, then they are certainly good enough for the people you love and the people you work with.

Thoughts to Ponder

- When complimented, a sincere "thank you" is the only response required.
- Spend less time worrying who is right and more time deciding what's right.
- Did anyone ever tell you not to *major* in *minor* things?
- A good nature will always supply the absence of beauty, but beauty cannot supply the absence of good nature.

"Take your life in your hands and what happens? A terrible thing: no one to blame!"

—*Erica Jong*

Growing up and blossoming into maturity certainly takes a great deal more than just reaching an older age. Even though you live every day one at a time, learning to enjoy one moment at a time is essential. You need to accept and learn from the hardships that come your way. If, and when, you reach maturity, it means that you have developed into what you are not only from your good experiences, but from your tough ones also. Taking charge and being emotionally sensitive encompasses the courage to face life's challenges and the intelligence to accept the unchangeable. The Alcoholics Anonymous fellowship shares a common prayer that states, "God grant me the serenity to accept the things I cannot change, the courage to change the things I can, and the wisdom to know the difference." That says it all. Remember, in order to be reasonably happy in this life, try to understand human behavior even though it continues to mystify and frustrate you. Having faith and accepting that you are who you are is a wonderful thing.

Thoughts to Ponder

- Believe in yourself, no matter what you choose.
- Wasn't it wonderful to find out that when you keep a winning attitude, you can never lose?
- Decide what today will be like because it is you who ultimately chooses what kind of day you will have.
- Remain open, flexible, and curious, and never give anyone a fruitcake for a present.

"All that is necessary to make this world a better place to live is to love."

—*Unknown*

The love given to you from your parents was not something they thought about, planned, or talked about. Love was something they just gave in their everyday actions as parents. They showed you, as Mother Teresa did, that love is found in the sweeping of a floor, cleaning a sink, caring for someone ill, or offering encouragement with a comforting hug. Without a second thought or without trying, they taught you the greatest and most lasting lesson of your life: loving and caring actions are far more important than spoken words. They are the qualities and actions that you live and act upon, day in and day out. It takes hard work, persistence, and patience to help your children develop a good self-image. And showing your love is the most important thing you can do to ensure their happiness and to make the world a better place.

Thoughts to Ponder

- Did you know a person's true character is revealed by what he does when no one is watching?
- Children aren't going to welcome being disciplined, but someday they will welcome the resultant good character traits.
- Let your children overhear you saying complimentary things about them to other adults.
- Rachel, age ten: "If you want to learn to love better, you should start with a friend who you hate."

"To nurture my soul and to fulfill my soul's purpose, I must learn from every event in my life. I must come to realize that every experience has within it a seed of a tremendous gift."

—*John Gray, Ph. D.*

When adversity drops in on your life, can you dig deep within your soul and draw out the best in you? That best consists of a combination of your capacity to forgive, have patience, be tolerant, be compassionate, and be generous; this is your soul strength. As you learn to expand and draw on your soul strengths, you will become more dependent on them in times of need. As you learn to be patient, tolerant, forgiving, and to have faith in a higher being, your ability to cope with life's problems will increase. The most important thing to remember is at the center of soul strength lies your faith in a higher being. Even with all the soul strength you might have and are able to muster up, it is a must to have a relationship with your God. Without this relationship you will continue to encounter endless problems of dealing with adversity.

Thoughts to Ponder

- Why is it that no one is perfect until you fall in love?
- I was taught to learn from and respect my elders, but it keeps getting harder to find one.
- I've learned to cherish all my memories, even the bad ones, for they are the "bricks and mortar" of who I am!
- Have faith; if it weren't for death, sometimes life would be unbearable.

"Love what you love with passion, but remember, love can also be nurtured by solitude."
—Leo Buscaglia

Loving relationships have emotional extremes. They challenge your patience, your understanding, and your resources. They also heighten your perceptions, passion, energy, and vitality. Signs of good relationships are those of wanting to be together all the time and sharing everything together. But no matter how much you love and care for someone, you should always find some time apart from each other. Someone once said, "A relationship should be like a moving sea between the shores of your souls. You should sing and dance together and be joyous, but each one of you should have some time to be alone." You need time to grow separately if you care about growing together. Time alone is well spent, especially when your love and passion can be re-nurtured with that solitude.

Thoughts to Ponder

- If you are patient in one moment of anger, you will escape a hundred days of sorrow.
- Just because two people argue it doesn't mean they don't love each other, and just because they don't argue doesn't mean they do love each other.
- Ask yourself, *What can I do today to make sure that the best things will happen?*
- Tender moments and lasting memories are most often the result of sharing simple things.

> *"Safety is the unsafe path you can take, as it can keep you numb and sad. People are caught by surprise when it is time to die and they have allowed themselves to live so little."*
>
> —*Steven Levine*

Remember your first love? You couldn't eat and sleep, and it was a tough time when weird thoughts kept you from being rational. You were wonderfully miserable and totally out of control, and everything seemed perfect, magical, and full of tenderness, laughter, and surprise. As time passed, what happened to that joy of your love? Did you outgrow it? Where and why did it vanish? The answer could be that you have forgotten that love is serious but not all that serious. You can bring back those magical times if you can get by your predictability and return to illogical reasoning. Step outside of that comfort zone and rekindle the happy days. You can remain true to your love by never allowing yourself to forget the laugher, humor, and surprise that was so much a part of your first love experience.

Thoughts to Ponder

- Love is an irresistible desire to be irresistibly desired.
- Love is what makes two people sit in the middle of a bench when there's plenty of room at both ends.
- Love doesn't make the world go 'round, it makes the ride worthwhile.
- Remember, there are either two winners or none.

"When you meet someone new, think, If I demonstrated love toward him or her, how would it affect my feelings toward them? The more you do this, the more loving and sensitive you become, and other people are changed simply by being loved."

—*Unknown*

We build the foundation of our home life each and every day, and it essential to realize the home we have built is the home we have to live in. If given another chance to build that foundation, what would you do differently? To avoid the problem of regret, it is essential to rehearse and practice loving behavior every day. The more you practice loving, caring, and sharing, the more you will become sensitive and aware of the love that surrounds you. Love begets love! Don't wait until the threat of death to pay attention to love and then try to make it a priority. When we are in pain, if someone is there for us and loving us, it is then we have received the greatest gift in the world, and we ultimately hurt a lot less. The same is true for those we love. Once you have a solid foundation built with a framing of care and a roof of gratitude, the warmth and love will bounce from the walls.

Thoughts to Ponder

- Life is a do-it-yourself project. Your attitudes and the choices you make today build the "house" you live in tomorrow. Build wisely!
- Have you ever noticed you always think of the right thing to say when it's too late?
- I hope the sun is shining just for you and the birds are singing their very best songs.
- Keep pouring out kindness and love—God won't let them run dry.

"If you haven't forgiven yourself for something, how can you forgive others?"

—*Dolores Huerta*

We all want to put our best foot forward and, as the Army used to say for recruiting, "Be all you can be." Striving to do your best is what life is all about. We are not perfect, we do make mistakes, and we do have small imperfections that mar our image. Keep in mind, they are not permanent; some can be changed and some are reversible. But first you need to forgive yourself as you would forgive others. You may find that to forgive oneself is to set a prisoner free and then discover the prisoner was you. Human imperfection is not a sickness, and very few people, if any, die from their imperfections. When you make errors in judgment, you are allowed to try again to improve those decisions and behaviors. Remember this: you don't always have to be right. Forgive yourself; give it another try, be persistent in your efforts to improve, learn from your mistakes, but don't be destroyed by them.

Thoughts to Ponder

- Did you know that the bridge you burn today could be the one you want to cross tomorrow?
- Never underestimate the power of words to heal and reconcile relationships.
- Don't point a finger—lend a hand.
- Never waste an opportunity to tell someone you care for them, but keep in mind flattery can be fancy dishonesty.

"The only sense that is common in the long run is the sense of change...And we all instinctively avoid it."
—E. B. White

Some say the only thing constant in life is the rate of change. Since life's situations are never experienced in the same way twice, they often confound and challenge us. Every new situation at home or work calls for unique behaviors and a full use of our rational and intuitive selves commonly called instinct and common sense. With age and experience, our reactions are different to perceived similar situations. Old habits, styles, and attitudes no longer seem to serve the new demands at hand. The good thing is that now you have to discover novel, ingenious ways to deal with your new challenges. Thinking you can handle it in the same old way and fearing a change in approach can lead to unsuccessful and unhappy results. Change may be difficult, but the results may be wonderful—try it, you'll like it!

Thoughts to Ponder

- Want success? Show up, pay attention, ask questions, and never give up.
- Think twice before you ask for or give advice.
- "There are no secrets to success: Don't waste time looking for them. Success is the result of perfection, hard work, learning from failure, loyalty to those for whom you work, and persistence." -General Colin Powell
- Change is inevitable, except from a vending machine!

"The adventurous life is not one exempt from fear, yet one that is lived in full knowledge of fears of all kinds is one in which we go forward in spite of our fears."
—*Paul Tournier*

There are certain risks and fears involved in moving outside of your comfort zone, in changing old habits, or in striving for closer relationships. When we take risks and acknowledge the need for dependency on others it's frightening. These ventures outside our comfort zone make us vulnerable, where we can easily be hurt or disappointed, especially in a new relationship. Wouldn't it be nice if you could just open yourself to others without fears or risk? Why not acknowledge the fear, take the risk, open up, and tell that special person that you care? In other words, just fly where you have not flown before. Oh, and you might consider using your Bible as a how-to guide.

Thoughts to Ponder

- Giving in is an important kind of giving when people love each other.
- Did you know you could multiply happiness by dividing it?
- Grief can take care of itself, but to get the full value of joy, you must have somebody to divide it with.
- Take the risk, challenge the fear, have faith in the Lord, and remember, with Him at your side you can fight off any feelings of fear.

> *"A true romantic feeling is not a desire to escape life, but to prevent life from escaping you."*
> —*Thomas Clayton Wolfe*

Have you been taking your loved one for granted lately? Has the novelty and spontaneity been replaced with predictability, habit, and routine? Are those once exciting and provocative things now predictable and routine? Someone once told me, "No one falls in love by choice; it is by chance. And no one stays in love by chance, it is by work." Fortunately, love and romance are easy to rekindle with freshness and surprise. So, don't let the romantic, happy life escape from you; prevent it by dreaming up some crazy things to spice it up. Dinner at a different restaurant, possibly a romantic one, candlelit quiet time, maybe a greeting at the door in a new outfit, or some inexpensive nonrefundable airline tickets to exotica. Remember, those true romantic feelings can fade a little but with a little help can be rekindled. Deep inside the magic is never gone; all you have to do is recreate it. Think about it and then decide which escape route from predictability you will take to resurrect those old romantic feelings.

Thoughts to Ponder

- It is not in doing what you like, but in liking what you do that is the secret of happiness.
- The most important thing you can do for your children is to love their mother.
- Remember that at times there some things that count that can't be counted and at times there are things that can be counted that don't count.
- Looking on the bright side of life will never cause eyestrain.

"One forgives to the degree that one loves."
—La Rochefoucauld

Do you burden yourself with guilt for the mistakes you made in the past? Maybe you worry and have regrets for some poor decisions you've made at home, at work, or in social and personal situations. Usually, you punish yourself way out of proportion as to the wrongs you may have done. One day you will need to stop being your own harshest judge and accept forgiveness from others as well as forgiving yourself. A forgiving person is a loving person, but forgiving oneself seems to be the most challenging. When you finally can, the results are rewarding; no more self-imposed pity, no bogus guilt or regrets to carry around. It's all about getting up, moving forward, and getting on with your life. Sometimes you just have to let it go.

Thoughts to Ponder

- If you're busy judging people, you have no time to love them.
- Always carry a bandage to remind you to heal hurt feelings—yours or someone else's.
- You can find the county of forgiveness and the town of happiness in your state of mind.
- Children need love, especially when they don't deserve it.

"No one grows old by living, only by losing interest in living."

—Unknown

Attitude affects everything you do, both personally and professionally. It reflects who you are, the aging process, and your interest in living. With just one life, it's up to you to keep an interest in living boldly and thus delaying the aging process. Since you cannot be 100% positive all of the time, the effort to adjust your attitude will take commitment, hard work, and continuous effort. Increasing your positive side means dealing with your negative/pessimistic thoughts and valuing the importance of friendships and supportive help during your struggle with negative thoughts. Negativity can be decreased by balancing your work with the time you spend on those needs that make you feel relaxed and happy, such as reading, walking, listening to music, or just meditating. Increase your optimism and build up your positive attitude muscles by slowing down, analyzing the facts with rational thinking. Finally you must act to settle problems even if it means direct conflict with your loved ones until you work out your disagreements. Remember: resolving a problem will relieve your stress, improve you optimistic side, and decrease your pessimism much more quickly and effectively than just complaining about them. It all begins with you putting your positive attitudes into action.

Thoughts to Ponder

- A man should not strive to eliminate his complexes, but rather to get into accord with them.
- Did you know that the courage to be is the courage to accept oneself in spite of being unacceptable?
- Memorize the Latin words carpe diem, which means to seize the day.
- Before you criticize someone, walk a mile in his shoes. That way, if he gets angry, he'll be a mile away—and barefoot.

"We tend to forget that happiness doesn't come as a result of getting something we don't have, but rather of recognizing and appreciating what we do have."
—*Frederick Koenig*

Have you ever attempted to explain happiness? Because it's such a very personal thing, happiness is almost impossible to define. For some people, happiness and inner peace come easily and in many cases can only be brought on by some special circumstance. I hope for you that happiness comes with the ordinary things, such as a dinner with friends, a walk in the park, a good conversation, watching the stars at night, or receiving a hug from your children and grandchildren. Since we are all different, what makes one person happy could have the opposite effect upon another. What makes you happy? Try to recognize it, and most of all you should try to appreciate it.

Thoughts to Ponder

- Don't mistake activity for achievement. Looking busy does not equal productiveness.
- Just as your eyes are, your words are also windows to your heart.
- You make a living by what you get, you make a life by what you give. Always remember that it is more blessed to give than to receive.
- Appreciate this little bit of happiness! Spread crunchy peanut butter on some gingerbread man cookies for a late-night snack.

"An ounce of discretion is worth more than a pound of knowledge."

—Unknown

When you are willing to have a little discretion, to postpone your demands, and to repress angry feelings (at least temporarily), that is when you truly value another's feelings. Holding your tongue in many cases is the better part of valor. This is especially true when you know there is no winning, and if you did have your say or the last word, it could possibly lose the respect of your friends. Using discretion will allow you to stop using and blaming other people as a means to your own end. It should not be a surprise to you if those individuals you verbally abused remain damaged and broken for years, if not forever. The lack of discretion is a distortion of basic decency, but when you show discretion, it shows you have truly gained the knowledge of friendship and love.

Thoughts to Ponder

- Did you know the strength of a man isn't in how respected he is at work? It's in how respected he is at home.
- The strength of a man isn't how many buddies he has. It's how good a buddy he is with his kids.
- Conscience is God's built-in warning system. Be very happy when it hurts you and be very worried when it doesn't.
- Never take problems to bed with you, for they make very poor bedfellows.

"Without forgiveness, life is governed by an endless cycle of resentment and retaliation."
—*Robert Assagioli*

We spend so much time and energy trying to get back at others or browbeating ourselves over past mistakes in judgment. It's a wonder any of us can even move under such a weight of guilt or resentment. Striking a balance in forgiving ourselves as well as others is the key to restful nights. We must learn not to be self-possessed by guilt while learning to forgive those who always try to make us feel guilty. Someone once told me, "If you want to be able to forgive others, you need to write the words 'I forgive me' on a piece of paper and keep saying the words over and over until you get the message." Then throw it away, burn it, or flush it—anything to be rid of it. If you falter, repeat the process. Remember, it isn't always enough to be forgiven by others—sometimes you have to learn to forgive yourself. End that cycle of resentment and retaliation.

Thoughts to Ponder

- It's better to die with a good name than to live with a bad one.
- Isn't it great to know achievement is based on not letting what you're doing get to you before you get to it?
- At all cost find ways to become more like Christ. Pursue the things of God and you won't be disappointed.
- You cannot judge a tree or a person by one season. How they grow and mature ultimately determines the essence of who they are.

"Obstacles are those things you see when you take your eyes off your goal."

—Unknown

We learn best from our role models, and we normally remember and admire the obstacles they overcome and their achievements. Relationships with role models and peers and how they influence our character development are primary in achieving our life's goals. Just how much influence they have, however, will always remain a mystery. If and when you are able to appreciate and take advantage of all the things that role models contributed in bringing you to maturity, you will have realized one of life's great intentions. For your part, you should welcome the mystery and respect that which has made you successful. I often remember a sign I read once that said, "While rambling through this world, brother, whatever be your goal, keep your eye upon the doughnut and not upon the hole." If your role model is a good one, you will learn to adjust your attitude and behavior to be a 110% person.

Thoughts to Ponder

- Never, never give up and always act as if it were impossible to fail.
- Do you realize that time is more valuable than money because time is irreplaceable?
- You are like a tea bag: you're not worth much until you have been through some hot water.
- When asked, "What do you think about when you strike out?" Babe Ruth said, "I think about hitting homeruns."

> *"Learn to laugh at your troubles and you'll never run out of things to laugh at."*
>
> —Lyn Karol

Isn't it strange how you tend to keep a record of the bad things that take place in your life while you so readily forget the good? To change this natural phenomenon, try gathering up as many memories of the good old days, the happy experiences, and fun times you've had, write them down, and place them in a memory jar. You now have your antidote to fight the fight. Trust me, those happy memories will come in handy during the times when things are not going well. During the rough times you need to laugh at the circumstances, the situation, and draw on your happier memories by reaching into your memory jar. Turning those painful experiences into positive ones is not easy, but the memory jar theory, in addition to a little humor and laughter, goes a long way. Keep a record of the times you've triumphed over misfortune; it will be your assurance that you can do so again, and those records will serve as a reservoir of strength when you most need it.

Thoughts to Ponder

- Did you know that taking time to play is the secret of perpetual youth?
- A man needs some stormy weather from time to time to remind him that he's not really in charge of anything.
- Happiness is when you have enough trials to make you strong, enough sorrow to keep you human, enough hope to make you happy, and enough money to buy Christmas gifts.
- Life is like a roll of toilet paper. The closer it gets to the end, the faster it goes.

"Vanity is so secure in the hearts of us that everyone wants to be admired—even I who says this, and you who read this."

—Blaise Pascal

Behavioral scientists tell us that compliments affect behavior far more powerfully than criticism. Yet we brandish criticism and negative comments, never understanding the repellent power of our negative comments or sour attitude. We are quick to criticize, yet we are so guarded with our praise. Try to remember that a positive anything is better than a negative nothing. How nice it is to bask in the warmth and approval of someone we respect. Without compliments, our personal dignity becomes seriously endangered. If someone's new outfit looks great, what harm can come from saying so? If someone is doing a good job, it can only reinforce the person to tell him or her how they are appreciated. Praise, like love, is only meaningful when freely shared.

Thoughts to Ponder

- When things go wrong, don't go wrong with them.
- Did you know that when you think and act cheerfully, you will feel cheerful and so will those around you?
- No one makes it alone! Have a grateful heart and be quick to acknowledge those who help you.
- Try forgiving by practicing forgiveness.

> *"It is not our toughness that keeps us warm at night, but our tenderness, which makes others want to keep us warm."*
>
> —*Harold Lyon*

When you have been ill treated or hurt by others, it is easier to show your tough side rather than your understanding, tender side. You act cool, calm, and collected when in fact you are very intimidated and leery of showing your real feelings. In fact, you are fearful of being honest and letting down your guard since it may open yourself to deeper relationships. There is a certain element of risk in seeking closeness with others and in acknowledging your dependence and trust in them. And it seems impossible to open yourself to someone without risk, especially when the risk can be a stepping stone or a stumbling block. On the positive side, your loved one may reciprocate with the warmth and tenderness you so desire. When you are a positive thinker, you will recognize the possible negatives, but you will refuse to dwell on them.

Thoughts to Ponder

- Try to keep love in your heart, because a life without love is like a sunless garden when the flowers are dead.
- When you are looking for a relationship, a job, or an apartment, you should ask your friends to help.
- Concern should drive you into action and not into depression.
- Grandpa and Grandma always know just what to say, even when it is nothing at all.

"I am only one, but still I am one. I cannot do everything, but still I can do something. I will not refuse to do the something I can do."
—Helen Keller

Some cultures teach that "you are the perfect you, no one can be a better you, no matter how much they so desire." It's a fact, no one can be a better you than you, but with faith and a positive attitude, you can influence and improve the overall you and your destiny. Your attitude is the window through which you must see the world, and the positive or negative response to situations determines your happiness. To make positive advances, it is essential to accept new challenges, get rid of the fear of failure, and understand that the choices you make today will shape your future. Simply said, you are not in competition with anyone; you are one of a kind, and you have something to offer that no one else has. To refuse to take charge and think with a negative attitude is not only a tragedy for you but for the world.

Thoughts to Ponder

- Give people more than they expect and do it cheerfully.
- God is a friend who knows all your faults and loves you anyway.
- Did you know silence is sometimes the best answer, and a wise man is one who thinks twice before saying nothing?
- The Philosopher Henri Louis Bergson once said, "To exist is to change, to change is to mature, to mature is to go on creating oneself endlessly."

"God must have realized humans need to be connected with the past, so he gave us memories."
—*Unknown*

Sometimes we think our personal worthiness and value to others decreases with age. In fact, growing old can be a wonderful experience, and with the proper planning and a positive outlook, your retirement days can be great. Talking to an elderly person who has a huge smile with a positive attitude and yet reminisces about happy days gone by is inspiring. And it's invigorating to be around those who are focused on the future, yet can reminisce about the "good ole days" without dwelling on them. A common topic expressed by the elderly is love. Love appears to be the centerpiece and the one common thread in each of their lives from cradle to grave. Be sure and strengthen your loving recollections by filling up your memory jar abundantly with them. The more you accumulate, the deeper the well will be to draw from later. In response to the question, "What are your needs in this later stage of life?" a lovely and wise eighty-year-old person said, "All I need and ever needed was someone to love and someone to love me. Nothing is changed."

Thoughts to Ponder

- Live a good, honorable life. Then when you get older and think back, you'll get to enjoy it a second time.
- The future belongs to those who believe in the beauty of their dreams.
- Did you know that when you have a purpose to fulfill and a dream to follow, God has opened your eyes and called you by name?
- Ask yourself at the end of the day, *Did I help someone to feel joy, laughter, or at least a smile?*

> *"The truth is more important than the facts, and trust is based on faith."*
>
> —*Frank Lloyd Wright*

Wouldn't you like to count on people to be honest, reliable, and just? It would be nice if they were always sincere and responsible. But sadly, this is not always true, and at times a leap of faith is required. You sometimes have to take a risk and rely on the honesty and sincerity of those you are dealing with even though you know they are imperfect and vulnerable. The West Point Cadet Maxim states, "Risk more than others think is safe. Care more than others think is wise. Dream more than others think is practical. Expect more than others think is possible." Truth and trust are built on faith and start at home. But never forget, what goes around comes around, and at times you must call upon your ability to forgive and restore your faith in human nature by setting the example.

Thoughts to Ponder

- Did you know that a little dispute could injure a great friendship?
- Trust implies forgetting the past and moving forward or just trying again.
- Every person should have a special cemetery plot in which to bury the faults of friends and loved ones.
- Ole southern prayer of faith: "O Lord, help me to understand that you ain't goin' to let nuttin' come my way that You and me together can't handle."

"Happiness is the interval between periods of unhappiness."

—*Don Marquis*

Most of our sadness and traumas in life come through loss, death, divorce, lost job, failing health, financial setbacks, broken hearts, or friendships. We were happy and then we are sad or unhappy. For most of us there is no way to avoid these situations since they exist as part of the reality of human existence. However, the only lasting trauma in life is the one we suffer when we don't learn from the experience and make some sort of positive change. We know that the sadness will pass and happy days will soon return. And in time the pain will subside, the wounds will heal, and you will discover the all-important truth: the most valuable thing we will ever possess is life itself.

Thoughts to Ponder

- God's promises are like the stars: the darker the night, the brighter the stars shine.
- Get in the driver's seat; don't be a passenger in your own life.
- When you are blue, wear audacious underwear under your most solemn business attire.
- There is more in us than we know. If we can be made to see it, perhaps, for the rest of our lives, we will be unwilling to settle for less."

"When you play, you should play without reason, and there must be no reason for it. Play is its own good reason."
—Lin Yutang

Too often we leave playing to our children and we enjoy watching the great satisfaction they get from it. It's too bad that adult games are taken too seriously and for the most part are structured for winning. Children's games are so much more enjoyable because youngsters play just for the joy of it. When you play as an adult, the sole purpose should be to have fun and to be diverted and amused for a while outside the realm of your normally structured life. Spontaneous and creative play can help you relate to people and things in new ways. And with spontaneity you will discover a positive side of yourself that celebrates life without trying to figure out every little problem. Get un-serious, leap outside those guards you've built around you, and quit being a stick in the mud. Play and have some fun. Be spontaneous and try taking a hot air balloon ride, celebrate your pet's birthday, introduce yourself to your neighbors, get away to an exotic location, or maybe send a handwritten letter instead of that e-mail.

Thoughts to Ponder

- If you want breakfast in bed, sleep in the kitchen.
- Bring your lunch to work once a week and make a date with yourself to enjoy it outside.
- Isn't it great to know the burden you carry will lighten when you laugh at yourself?
- Recall them as often as you wish—happy memories never wear out.

"Problems are only opportunities in work clothes."
—*Henry J. Kaiser*

There are some old adages that state, "If you want something strongly enough, it's yours for the taking," and "Where there's a will, there's a way." When feeling sorry for yourself, you might rebut someone by saying, "Easy for you to say that," or "You haven't walked in my shoes." Well, you do have the power to improve things or take control of the situation, but you need to have the will and the persistence to do so. Solutions come on the heels of need, but they do not materialize on their own, and that means putting on your work clothes and being persistent. The question is, do you really want the success badly enough to do the soul searching and hard work necessary to acquire it, or are you just kidding yourself, thinking you want it? Taking those desires and turning them into opportunities is the only way you will find out!

Thoughts to Ponder

- You can be anything you want to be, have anything you desire, and accomplish anything you set out to accomplish if you will hold to that desire with singleness of purpose.
- Life is simpler when you plow around the stumps.
- It is necessary to learn that what you hope to do with ease must first be done with diligence.
- When you think you should give up on life, search for a place of worship that you truly enjoy…and then attend faithfully.

> *"Prejudgments become prejudices only if they are not reversible when you receive new knowledge."*
> —George Bancroft

Disagreement can actually enhance a relationship. You may not agree with this statement, especially when you are in the midst of a heated argument and you think you are correct. But what makes you unique as an individual is your diversity of opinion or prejudgments, the way you express them, and the way you perceive the world. When you receive additional information with an open mind and can change your attitude and opinion, it indicates a well-balanced individual with perfectly acceptable behavior. And if you encounter those who do not accept change no matter what, all is not lost because it is possible for mature adults to disagree completely and still live and work together. Take note of the end result (good or bad) of your last disagreement, the way you handled yourself, and any positive or negative approaches you used. Use this new knowledge wisely and it could lead to you being a better person for it.

Thoughts to Ponder

- Patience is a quality you admire in the driver behind you. Scorn is what you think about in the one ahead of you.

- When you argue and get angry, you have the right to be angry, but this doesn't give you the right to be cruel.

- Ask yourself, *Did I think of someone, anyone, today in a more positive light?*

- It's easy to be deceived about yourself, but did you know God sees the right and the wrong in you even when you try to hide it?

"Communication is the art of talking with each other, not to each other."

—Unknown

Contrary to popular belief, communication is an acquired skill and not a natural by-product of two people coming together. It takes the same skills in your personal life as in your working environment. The major components or skills to tune up on when talking with each other are listening and showing concern. Things that you think go without saying or that you think are understood can build up a mountain of miscommunication if not said or heard. You need to communicate—you cannot hear what the other person is not saying, and they cannot hear what you do not say. Sometimes, when you or they finally do hear what's being said, it's too late. To talk with each other, you should say what you mean and what you clearly feel without deception or disguise.

Thoughts to Ponder

- Be tactful and never alienate anyone on purpose.
- Learn to disagree without being disagreeable.
- The real art of communication is not only to say the right thing in the right place but, more importantly, to leave unsaid the wrong thing at the tempting moment.
- Ask yourself at the end of the day, *Have I attempted to remove a little of the rust that is corroding my relationships?*

"No one seeks out bitter fruit. The same is true with bitter people."

—Unknown

When you harbor bitterness, it only ends up souring your own life. Try to remember when you have unceasing negativity that it will lead to further isolation from friends and coworkers. If you turn a bitter face to the world, for whatever reason, you can expect little else in return. If, however, you face adversity with a sense of humor and hold to a lifestyle of gratitude for what you have, you're likely to find people responding to you in the same way. Experience tells us that what we get back from life is usually what we give. So we are raised and encouraged to treat others as we would like to be treated and that we should do unto others as we would have others do unto us. Every day bears its own gifts, and all you have to do is untie the ribbons and keep a positive attitude of gratitude.

Thoughts to Ponder

- Your words are windows to your heart.
- Do not start each day anticipating trouble or worrying about what may never happen. Keep in the sunlight.
- Do not judge others where you have not compassion.
- The most valuable gift you can give another is a good example.

"We don't make mistakes. We just have learnings."
—Anne Wilson Schaef

Confronting life's daily ups and downs at times seems overwhelming. When seemingly impossible problems at work or home arise, you can choose either to exercise control over your life or lose precious time complaining and whining as a perceived victim of your circumstances. When you make a mistake and stagnate yourself in self-pity, you are taking one step forward and then two backwards. Someone once told me they were neither an optimist nor pessimist, but a possibilist. If you can learn something from your mistakes and go forward, going backward will only be a memory. Your best option is learning and moving on. It's definitely far more productive and more exciting than hanging on to the "Woe is me" syndrome.

Thoughts to Ponder

- Shower those you care for with genuine praise.
- If you are ever granted the privilege of leadership, you should be there for your people at all times.
- When you greet a friend and ask how they are, if they are saying, "Fine!" with a scowl, try replying with, "Well, then why don't you tell your face?"
- At the end of the day ask yourself, *Have I gone through the day fretting over what I don't have rather than celebrating the things I do have?*

"A wise person's heart guides their mouth, and their lips promote instruction. Pleasant words are a honeycomb, sweet to the soul and healing to the bones."

Proverbs 16:23–24

The person who tells you they never get angry is either a liar or a potential time bomb. If you are lucky, you can hold your temper, get mad or angry for five minutes, blow off some steam, and get over whatever caused the problem. A minute of thought is worth more than an hour of debate or angry talk, and when you have no anger it has been proven that you will have no ulcers and no loss of sleep. In some people, when anger is repressed, it eventually explodes with greater intensity than can be imagined. It gets further out of proportion than the original provocation, leaving in its wake a greater resentment and, in some cases, deteriorating health. If you repress your anger, it always festers and finds expression in hurt to yourself and others. Anger can't be ignored or wished away, so why not accept it as a natural human experience to be dealt with and expressed in a healthy manner? Keep a tight rein on yours!

Thoughts to Ponder

- In disagreements, deal with the current situation. Don't bring up the past.
- One reason a dog has so many friends is that he wags his tail instead of his tongue.
- Did you know if you smile when you pick up the phone, the caller hears it in your voice?
- At the end of the day, ask yourself, *Have I forgiven others for being less than perfect?*

"It may not be that you can't see the solution. Maybe it is that you can't see the problem."

—G. K. Chesterton

Too often when confronted with a problem, we seek to find the perfect solution. Seeking the perfect answer usually results in frustration and sometimes drives us to distraction rather than a required positive action. Every problem will have as many solutions as there are creative individuals dealing with it. Slowing down and using the most powerful resource of thinking things out is the best way to approach problems, not flying off the handle and trying the first thing that comes to mind. A healthy individual is one who has the most viable alternatives available (not necessarily the best) for whatever perceived problem they have. The most difficult thing to remember is that your problems always have more than one solution, and taking your time and dealing with them head on in a positive manner is always the best approach.

Thoughts to Ponder

- The older you get, the better you will realize you are.
- As long as one keeps searching, the answers come.
- Failure is the condiment that gives your final solution its flavor.
- The trouble with the guy who talks too fast is that he often says something he hasn't thought of yet.

"We cannot tell what may happen to us in the strange medley of life. But we can decide what happens in us—how we can take it, what we can do with it—and that is what really counts in the end."

—*Joseph Fort Newton*

Adversity requires some sort of action. Don't waste time asking yourself, "Why me?" It only produces needless, meaningless conflict, loss of sleep, and ulcers. Instead, ask yourself, "What should I do now?" Since most problems always have more than one solution, if you take your time and deal with it head on and in a positive manner, you will take control in deciding what happens. When you are in control of your decisions and actions, you do away with the self-pity and meaningless blaming of others for your situation.

You and only you are accountable for your resolve. Remember, adversity is actually what helps you to grow, change, and survive, and taking control of it is what really counts in the end.

Thoughts to Ponder

- Be even more loving to others when the world is being cruel to you.
- Fix what's broken, whether it's a machine or a personal problem. Friends and family don't need to be burdened by problems that you could have corrected.
- If you think you are entitled to happiness, you must not only earn it for yourself, but also dispense it.
- Growing old is inevitable, but growing up is optional.

"Love has nothing to do with what you are expecting to get, only with what you are expecting to give—which is everything."

—Katharine Hepburn

The problem with loving unconditionally is meeting the condition of loving unconditionally. As time goes by, "conditions" change but, most importantly, you change, and it appears that unconditional loving is something only your puppy seems to be able to do. It has been said that to maintain love, two people must come together completely as one. In fact, almost the reverse is true. Only in growing separately can individuals grow together! It may be time not only to let your loved one grow, but maybe you should encourage it. When you do, you will find that your love for each other may just begin to grow stronger, and maybe, just maybe, you can come close to achieving unconditional love. An author and lecturer once talked about a contest he was asked to judge. The purpose of the contest was to find the most caring child. The winner was a four-year-old child whose next-door neighbor was an elderly woman who had recently lost her husband. Upon seeing the woman cry, the little boy went into the old woman's yard, climbed onto her lap, and just sat there. When his mother asked what he had said to the neighbor, the little boy said, "Nothing, I just helped her cry."

Thoughts to Ponder

- The best relationship is one where your love for each other is greater than your need for each other.
- "Do everything in love" (1 Corinthians 16:14).
- *We give dogs time we can spare, space we can spare, and love we can spare. And in return, dogs give us their all. It's the best deal man has ever made.*

> *"As long as one can admire and love, then one is young forever."*
>
> —*Pablo Casals*

No one looks forward to growing old, especially after they leave their teens. Recently when I returned from my high school reunion, I thought to myself, *The years have crept up on everyone so very fast, but not me, of course, because I still look and feel like a youngster.* In reality, the receding hairline, wrinkled skin, and slower pace are not the real reasons we may dread old age. In actuality, we fear the day when our loved ones stop planning with us and start planning for us. Stay young at heart forever, and remember that you and your parents will always remain the loving persons you are with the same needs despite the outer shell that might suggest otherwise. Even though the golden years are not what they are cracked up to be, we need to love and be loved until the day we die.

Thoughts to Ponder

- Always be nice to your children because they are the ones who will choose your rest home.
- The quickest way to receive love is to give love. The fastest way to lose love is to neglect it.
- God wants us to meet a few wrong people before meeting the right one so that when we finally do meet the right person, we know how to be grateful for that blessing.
- To affirm love and to hear about one's dignity and worth are to the soul as food is to the body.

"To love is to place your happiness in the happiness of another."

—*Gottfried Wilhelm Van Lubreitz*

How often do you place your own needs and desires over those of the people you love? A good way to determine how much you truly care for someone is to assess how high his or her happiness and welfare are on your priority list. For instance, do you place your own personal gains, needs, and desires over theirs? Do you postpone your success or personal desires so they can be content? Rearranging your priorities for others and true concern for their happiness is an indication of true love. However, giving someone your love is never an assurance that they'll love you back! Don't expect love in return; wait for love to grow in their hearts, and if it doesn't, be content that it grew in yours. During this year, take the time for an honest look at your behavioral priorities. You may be surprised to find your happiness in that of others.

Thoughts to Ponder

- Love starts with a smile, develops with a kiss, and ends with a tear.
- Take heed that there are persons that love you dearly, but simply do not know how to express or show their feelings.
- Grandma and Grandpa's influence in a child's life is forever love in that child's heart.
- Some of your most prized possessions are words that you have never spoken.

> "Life is our greatest possession and love its greatest affirmation."
>
> —*Leo Buscaglia*

When you treat people as they are, they will stay as they are. But if you treat them for what they might be, and might become, you might be surprised at the results. Affirm your love by showing it. If you treat people with love and respect and give them praise and encouragement, they can't help but become better. It may hurt to love someone and not be loved in return, but to love someone without the courage to show it is more painful. Share your greatest possession and announce your feelings of love. Affirming that love will help you in realizing that you are special and unique, and your uniqueness is one quality that attracts others. Remember, the giving of love is the best way of sharing yourself.

Thoughts to Ponder

- "Love is when my mommy makes coffee for my daddy and she takes a sip before giving it to him to make sure the taste is okay." Ryan, age 9
- Assert your love; do what needs doing when it needs to be done; don't procrastinate.
- *You can say any foolish thing to a dog, and the dog will give you a loving look that says, Wow, you're right! I never would've thought of that!*
- Isn't it comforting to know you're unique, just as others are?

> *"The past should not be used as an anvil for beating out the present and the future."*
> —Paul—Emile Borduas

It's as useless to drag old concerns and bring them into the present day as it is to fear the future. We all know people who are protesting, grumbling, whining, or complaining about past problems or perceived future problems. Who wants to be around that type of person? Stop analyzing everything and worrying about things that may or may not happen because of past mistakes. Begin to enjoy what is happening around you now. Those who believe in themselves and trust in the moment are those who find life most enjoyable. Remember that the past is a place to store memories, not regrets. The future should be full of promise, not apprehension. And the present is all you need.

Thoughts to Ponder

- Yesterday is history, tomorrow is a mystery, and today is a gift. That is why we call it the present.
- No one chooses his parents or childhood, but you can choose your own direction.
- It is far more impressive when others discover your good qualities without your help.
- You can't expect your sins to be forgiven when you haven't forgiven others. Try to remember that the noblest vengeance is to forgive.

"Problems are messages."
—*Shakti Gawain*

Over the years the problems you have encountered and overcome should have become great teachers. And the lessons learned should now allow you to make logical adjustments to similar or new situations. Physical pains are messages that mobilize your immune system, and inner pains are messages that alert your emotional system so you can take evasive action. In either case, some people look for instant relief by taking drugs, drowning themselves in alcohol, overeating, or oversleeping to suppress them. If you have learned anything from your previous experiences, you know these alternatives are not the answer when problem messages indicate your immediate attention. Drugs or alcohol will not wash away your problems; besides, when you wake or sober up, they will still be there. It's up to you! It's always your choice to take control of the situation or let it control you. Work on learning and growing from your prior problem messages, as they all have something to give. Remember, you don't stop learning until the moment you stop trying and always know that the knowledge you gain is a weightless treasure you will forever carry and draw from.

Thoughts to Ponder

- You have not learned anything until you have learned there is always something left to love.
- Always know that wherever you go, you take you with you. Be good to *you*.
- Why would anyone want to live on top of the mountain when all the happiness and growth occurs while climbing it?
- Eat one live toad the first thing in the morning and nothing worse will happen to you the rest of the day.

"Winning is overemphasized. The only time it is really important is in surgery and war."

—*Al McGuire*

Is it necessary to be right if it continually causes resentment and ill will? At home, work, and play, consideration is what most people need from us, not an "I'm right all the time" attitude. Being a real winner entails knowing when to speak your mind or when to be quiet, when to give in and when to stand firm, when to act or not to act, and when to set your limits or extend them. A key to strong relationships is the willingness to allow others to take center stage sometimes. Being mindful not only of your own needs but of others around you and putting them first is paramount in developing and/or essential in creating long-lasting relationships. Maybe you should be more concerned with what God thinks about you than what people think, and winning will take its course.

Thoughts to Ponder

- He who cannot forgive breaks the bridge over which he himself must pass.
- Being a winner means not quitting at the first sign of problems, or the second, or the next.
- The hardest part of your body to control is your tongue. If you can do this, you're almost perfect.
- Even though you want to win, it's not good sportsmanship to pick up lost golf balls while they are still rolling.

"The only justification we have to look down on someone is because we are about to pick them up."
—Jesse Jackson

Have you ever rushed to judgment? Do you know someone who has opinions about everything, even when they don't know anything about the subject? Some people spend a lot of time predicting, estimating, speculating, deciding, and criticizing, usually with little or no foundation. Well, don't you make the same mistake without examining your motives! When you start to feel you are better than others, remember the old Indian adage that says, "You can't understand anyone else until you have spent ample time in his moccasins," or "Before trying to fit into anyone else's moccasins, you should feel more comfortable in your own." The way to understand is to be an understanding person and keep your words soft and tender. This will help eliminate you from having to eat them and just maybe the moccasins won't hurt your feet.

Thoughts to Ponder

- Why is it that by the time a man is wise enough to watch his step, he's too old to go anywhere?
- Today you can lament over what your parents didn't give you when you were growing up, or you can feel grateful that they allowed you to be born.
- Stay clear of hatred and vengeance; they're the fuel that burns without producing energy and are a waste of time.
- Never argue with an idiot. They drag you down to their level and then beat you up with experience.

"Today if well lived, makes every yesterday a dream of happiness and every tomorrow a vision of hope."
—*Unknown*

Most of us tend to get so wrapped up in the trivialities of living that we forget to live. Today is the time for doing and giving, for going places, for spreading happiness, for accomplishing the things we've relegated to the land of "someday" or when the time is right. Take care to say a kind word to that little one who looks up to you in awe because that little person soon will grow up and leave. Don't fall into the mode of dull complacency that may lull you into the belief that you will always have tomorrow. Spend some time with your loved ones: your family, friends, neighbors, and coworkers. Don't wake up today and regret yesterday.

Thoughts to Ponder

- A glad heart gives you cheerful hopes for the future.
- Don't compare yourself to others. You will be judged individually on your own merits, not as a group on a comparison basis!
- Recipe for a happy home: Fill a house with equal parts of love, hope, and peace. Add the joy of children, the strength of older people, and the Spirit of Christ. Spread over all the blessings of contentment and season with the music of laughter and sprinkle with kisses. Add a crackling fire and serve with a great big welcome and much cheer.
- If you lend someone twenty dollars and never see that person again, it was probably worth it.

"Conditions are never just right. People who delay action until all factors are favorable do nothing."
—*Unknown*

At times it's easier to postpone searching for happiness until circumstances and conditions in your life are better. As you are aware, it's not always easy to be positive and find joy and happiness in yourself, let alone find it elsewhere. When you are at odds with others and are yet able to keep that good attitude, it becomes easier to look for the good in every situation. In personal confrontations try to be humorous and don't be afraid to praise. Don't have any expectations about how you should be treated, don't compare yourself to anyone else, and just be glad that you are who you are. Remember the most important trip you may take in life is meeting people halfway. So above all stop worrying about, *What's in it for me?* and start to think about what you can do to help others. Sometimes you have to leave your city of comfort and go into the rural zone of yourself. What you discover will be wonderful and that discovery will be yourself! Remember that you're a work in progress; keep a positive attitude and happiness will be yours.

Thoughts to Ponder

- Forgive those who have offended you, not for them, but for yourself.
- Remember that your courage will grow with the occasion.
- Don't jump to conclusions, run down your friends, sidestep responsibility, or push your luck.
- Life can never get you down once you have found the love of your Lord.

> *"You will never attempt anything if you think all possible objections must first be overcome."*
> —*Samuel Johnson*

Because of perceived complications, many of us choose to stay in our comfort zone and not actively participate in all that life has to offer. When you decide to move outside of your comfort zone and attempt to live life to the fullest, you quickly find out it is not always easy. So be assured that as long as you allow others into your life, a certain degree of conflict, confusion, anxiety, and emotional frustration will accompany it. In your quest you need to accept these facts. Love may also bring you some discomfort, sadness, and doubt, but don't let these thoughts or feelings cause you to shy away or to withdraw. Once you choose to take charge of these feelings and emotions, your life will be fuller. So deal with each emotion one at a time, knowing that some you will resolve and some you won't. And whether you win or lose, knowing that you tried is certainly better than staying in a comfort zone having not tried at all.

Thoughts to Ponder

- True faith and courage to overcome are like kites: an opposing wind raises them higher.
- Life is not dull and boring unless you approach life in a dull, boring fashion.
- When you are living life to the fullest, what you see in the mirror will delight you, and what others see in you will delight them.
- Why can't you accept your body's size and shape? It's uniquely yours.

"Anything worthwhile is worth waiting for."
—Unknown

Patience is something some of us have difficulty developing at home and in our working relationships. What about you? Are you the type who always demands to have action and answers immediately? Patience implies your willingness to bear suffering, endure delay in your life, and hang in there when things become difficult. Sometimes we overlook the fact that if we want fast action, correct answers, and permanent change, we must often have patience and wait. At the end of that patience trail you will receive strengthened commitments, ease of mind, and, best of all, the miracle of patience returned. Remember that throughout your life patience is the basic quality of which "forever-aftering" is made.

Thoughts to Ponder

- Take time to call your friends, even if it's only on their birthday.
- When will we learn that it is much easier in life to happily achieve than it is for us to achieve so we can be happy?
- Be patient with each other, making allowance for each other's faults because of your love. Read Ephesians 4:2.
- Have patience and know that if you are facing a fork in the road, you should keep your eyes peeled for God's road signs. He promises to guide you.

> *"You don't get to choose how you're going to die, or when. You can only decide how you're going to live now."*
> —*Joan Baez*

No matter how you choose to live today, keep your head high and your nose at a friendly level. If you choose to be a loving person today, what counts is not the number of hours you put in, but how much loving you put in the hours. So give away as much love as you can as freely as you can and without return expectations. If you are rejected, you will need the courage to rise up and try again. If you are hurt, you must have the confidence that you will heal, and if you feel devastated, you must muster up the human dignity to prevail, remembering that sad times may be blessings in disguise. Ask your Creator for the courage not to give up, even though you think it is hopeless. With that type of courage to meet whatever hindrances you may encounter along the way, you become more than just a reactor to your life. You are the actor who determines your course in life.

Thoughts to Ponder

- Nothing is carved in stone; you can change anything in your life if you want to badly enough.
- As you begin to give away love, your life will be filled with love and others will follow that path of love.
- Ask yourself, *Is anyone I met today happier because of me?*
- Wouldn't it be nice if whenever we messed up our life we could simply press "Ctrl-Alt-Delete" and start all over?

"People change and don't tell each other."
—*Lillian Hellman*

If you are truly alive, I am certain that you are going through the process of being reborn each and every day. On the surface you may appear unchanging, but beneath the surface alterations are going on, undetected and unappreciated. Since you accept that your physical body undergoes dramatic changes with time, you should accept the fact that your mind, tastes, opinions, beliefs, and dreams are also changing. Never assume anything permanent about yourself, your fellow workers, or the people you love, as change has no special time of its own. Its hour is always now. Remember that with each and every day that goes by, there is a lifetime of new beginnings for both them and you. To understand life you must look inward and backwards, but for you to live life to its fullest you must look forward.

Thoughts to Ponder

- If you aren't willing to work for your goals, don't expect others to.
- Keep your mind off the things you don't want to change by keeping it on the things you do want to change.
- Every mind is a room filled with archaic furniture. Clean out a corner of your mind and creative change will instantly fill it.
- A mind that is stretched by new experiences of influencing others can never go back to its old dimensions.

> *"There are many truths of which the full meaning cannot be realized until personal experience has brought it home."*
>
> —*John Stuart Mill*

In a loving relationship, sharing does not mean keeping a balance sheet of who is doing what and who is doing more or who is more understanding or caring. Keeping score belongs in competitive sport, not at work or in a mutually supportive relationship. The truth is, you cannot control time; you can only control yourself, and now is the time for expressing some unconditional love through caring and giving. As you begin to share your love with the world and the people in it, you will find that this love manifests itself and returns to you. The true meaning of love can be realized when the players are mature, caring, and they cease keeping score. When this happens, the contest is over and everyone can declare victory.

Thoughts to Ponder

- Follow the three R's: respect for self, respect for others, and responsibility for all of your actions.
- The more you share your love, the more love will come into your life.
- Sharing your love does not always demand a heavy sacrifice, only the willingness to make it happen.
- Blessed are you who hunger and thirst, for you are probably sticking to your diet.

"The bird of paradise alights only upon the hand that does not grasp."

—*John Berry*

Subscribing to the idea that you are truly and exclusively loved by your soul mate is a fantasy when, in fact, loving and being loved by many is the reality in life. Actually, you are capable of loving any number of people at the same time, which includes lovers, family, and friends. In your quest for love, don't be discouraged if it seems difficult to find, and don't shut love out of your life by thinking it's impossible. The quickest way to receive love is to give love; the fastest way to lose love is to hold it too tightly; and the best way to keep love is to give yours its wings. Seeking, searching, and grasping for love is not what attracts that paradise; it's when yours is given without any strings attached or unconditionally. Love is enriched, intensified, and whole when love becomes a give-and-take part of life and the give is more than the take. So accept it when given, and most of all, give yours freely and frequently without expectations.

Thoughts to Ponder

- Don't waste a minute trying to demonstrate or tell others the truthfulness of your love. If your actions do not vindicate themselves, you cannot vindicate them.
- What you achieve or fail to achieve in love is directly related to what you do or fail to do.
- Logic is a machine of the mind, as is love, and if it is used honestly it will bring out an honest conclusion.
- Try not to spend too much time looking for the right person to love or finding fault with those you already love; instead you should spend time perfecting the love you give.

"One more good man on earth is better than an extra angel in heaven."

—Chinese Proverb

The universal story of caring is written line by line with the simple acts of loving and caring for others and doing kindness for those who are having a hard time. As a good person, your act of kindness or caring may have more effect and power than you can realize. Even though you may consider them ordinary acts, they are more important to the soul than their simplicity might suggest. When you become active in the selfless treatment of others, you are forever enhancing yourself, and you will never be alone or unloved. As an angel in training and a friend, you should be fanatical in your friendships. The angel training manual states that a true friend cheers them when the world boos at them, dances when they get good news, and cries when they cry.

Thoughts to Ponder

- Grandparents add a great deal to a child's life by providing a gentle hug, an approving smile, encouragement, and a simple compliment.
- If you truly treasure a friendship, put more into the relationship than you take out.
- In every life situation it is better to give than to receive. Share the blame once in while, even if you don't own it.
- Have you ever wondered how a two-pound box of candy can make you gain five pounds? Maybe we should share the candy!

"Tears wash the sadness from the windows that shine on your soul."

—*Unknown*

Happiness is for those who cry, who hurt, who have searched, and for those who have tried. Many people have spent their lives with a negative outlook and are totally preoccupied with themselves, yet have never cried. With a good cry you can release the past and set your heart to a bright future. And if you can look at the sunset and still smile, you still have hope. You are mistaken if you believe that crying is a sign of weakness. A good healthy cry can be a sign of release and maturity; your tears are signs for others, showing your compassion and thoughtfulness. Clear eyes allow them to see your inner being, the true you. The real weakness in life is not accepting help from your friends and not allowing yourself access to the emotions expressed through your tears.

Thoughts to Ponder

- The difference between passion and passionate lies in your ability to share what you feel with others.
- Has anyone ever told you that you don't stop laughing because you grow old, you grow old because you stop laughing?
- Hold a good friend with both hands.
- Live well today, as it will soon be your yesterday.

"The life and love you create is the life and love you live."
—*Leo Buscaglia*

Part of your uniqueness is your diversified opinion when viewing your situation, the world, and the affection you have for others. Just as loving thoughts can bring you peace of mind, prejudgments can instill jealousy and envy and bring you strife, discontentment, and restless nights. To accept and love, there is no need to agree on all things all of the time. To keep your prejudgments from becoming prejudices, it's necessary to revise them when you are exposed to new facts and knowledge. Being able to create the type of life and love you want each day, you need to keep a positive, loving attitude. The bottom line is that it is possible for mature adults to disagree completely, get along, and still care for each other when the desire to love is there. The attitude you create is the life you live!

Thoughts to Ponder

- A man is never in worse company than when he flies into a rage and is beside himself.
- If you aren't giving from pure motives, you may not be able to count on getting the blessings you thought.
- Clear proof of the love you have for your Lord is when you genuinely show love to your fellow human beings.
- Always let your children and grandchildren know you love them just the way they are.

"Love is constant, it is we who are fickle. Love does guarantee, people betray. Love can always be trusted, people cannot."

—*Unknown*

Whenever you think there is an impasse or feel something is lacking in your personal life, the solution to the dilemma is usually found in taking some new form of action with your life. Even though love can be trusted, the usual ho-hum approach needs to be dropped, and you need to engage life today with a greater desire for enthusiastic love. Share yours with more tenderness, more patience, more forgiveness, and more gratitude. This poem tells of the ultimate attitude of gratitude and provides a way to start your day. Create your attitude of gratitude by starting your day and living it this way:

"I think I'll start today with a grin. I have nothing to lose, just friendship to win. If there were no reason for me to live today, God would have called me yesterday. I have many things to be happy for, and I will smile on them not searching for more."

Thoughts to Ponder

- Words, like angels, are powers that have invisible strength over us.
- Positive action has a way of reopening your heart and the hearts of others.
- Time is nature's way of keeping everything from happening at once.
- Why is it that when you talk to God, you're praying? However, when he talks to you, you're crazy.

"With so many spectacular colors in the world, it's a shame to make everything black and white."
—*Dennis R. Little*

Things are usually not all good or all bad, all right or all wrong, especially when dealing with life's problems. It is not that simple. When you insist on only black or white, you remove yourself from understanding the truth. At work and at home, try handling frustration and pressures by yielding a little rather than standing firm each time you encounter a difficult situation. Giving in does not imply giving up any more than being flexible is a sign of lacking conviction. If you mess up and make mistakes, it's not your parents' fault. When you make correct decisions, take a little less than your share of the credit. When you move on from black-and-white decisions to the color side for your decisions, learn from your choices. By giving in a little, you can get more than you ever dreamed. Try it!

Thoughts to Ponder

- Emotional swings can distort our perception of reality and are capable of making fools of us. Remember, if you are willing to slow down and wait before becoming judgmental, your reactions can be tempered.
- If you want to know what's in your heart, listen to your mouth.
- The good news is that the more we know God intimately, the more clearly we'll hear His whispered guidance.
- Isn't it frustrating when you know all the answers and nobody bothers to ask you the question?

> *"Caring at home and at work should not be a thing of words and fine talk. It should be a thing of action and sincerity."*
> —*Unknown*

Have you hurt someone's feelings lately by not showing your affection or created sadness in their life by not telling them of your love? Take heart! Life sometimes gives you a second chance to reprieve yourself, and it takes very little effort on your part to make others happy. All that's required is an educated heart, kindness mixed with honesty and sincerity, and a plan. Turn your plan into action by taking a little time each day to point out something positive about a friend or coworker. In this way, you certainly will have influenced someone's future today. Remind yourself of your plan each day by associating it to planting a garden with five rows of lettuce: lettuce be joyful, lettuce be caring, lettuce be kind, lettuce be positive, and lettuce truly love one another.

Thoughts to Ponder

- I've learned that no matter what happens or how bad it seems today, life does go on, and it will be better tomorrow.
- Good judgment comes from experience, and a lot of that comes from bad judgment.
- Sing a happy song because you rejoice in seeing someone today and give that person a big hug.
- Why is it that when you're driving and looking for an address, you turn down the volume on the radio?

"You and I are more important than our problems."
—*Unknown*

At times you may feel you are not appreciated and people do not recognize that you are truly remarkable and have valuable attributes. Even so, don't undermine your worth with a pity party or by comparing yourself with others. Now is the time when you need to reach way down inside your soul and call on your faith. When you have strong faith it makes a difference, and that difference makes you the special person you are. Faith is the one and only inexhaustible resource for positive reinforcement you have, and when you want to do things correctly or are striving to get the job done right, your faith can and will help carry you through. When you realize you are number one, that's the time when you can proudly wave your own personal flag, knowing all things are possible through faith.

Thoughts to Ponder

- Have faith, and if life happens to deliver a situation that you cannot handle, kindly put it in the SFGTD (Something for God to Do) box. It will be addressed in His time, not yours. Once the matter is placed into the box, do not hold onto it.
- Water your garden of life freely with patience and cultivate it with love.
- The poorest man I know is the man who has nothing but money.
- When you have silver hair, tin ears, a lead bottom, and a heart of gold, chances are you are a grandparent.

"One who lets slip by the opportunity to help or serve another misses one of the richest experiences life has to offer."

—*Pali Text*

Regardless of your relationship with your parents, you'll miss them when they're gone from your life. The same is true of loved ones and friends. Each day goes by with lost opportunities and postponements to express your genuine feelings. Even though your love is genuine and your intentions are good, you still make up reasons or excuses for not expressing them. Experience that special gift life has to offer when you know they know how you care. Even though it may not seem quite right, the mood may feel wrong, or you think there are more important things to do, now is the time! No excuses will do! Don't treat them like the book you have been meaning to read or the phone call you intend to make or the letter you plan to write. Express your feelings now and try to remember that it is never too late to turn over a new leaf and make that call. Keep the memory of those beautiful people in your life alive.

Thoughts to Ponder

- Don't forget that a person's greatest emotional need is to feel appreciated.
- You cannot do an act of kindness too soon, for you never know how soon it will be too late.
- Approach love and cooking with reckless abandonment.
- William Wordsworth once said, "The best portion of a good man's life are his little, nameless, forgotten acts of kindness and of love."

> *"Minds are like parachutes: they function only when they are open."*
>
> —*Unknown*

Most people are preoccupied with trying to figure out what life is all about. Isn't it amazing that you finally begin to figure it out once most of your life has slipped away and it seems like you are now cramming for the finals? No matter how bad your day is going there is always a lot to be thankful for if you take time to look for it. For example, I am sitting here thinking how nice it is that wrinkles don't hurt. If they did, wow! And if you haven't figured it out or don't have a clue, let me save you a lot of your life's most precious time! Life is what is happening while you waste time pondering what life is all about. Open up the parachute to your mind and live your life now; dissect it later.

Thoughts to Ponder

- You shouldn't go through life with a catcher's mitt on both hands. You need to be able to throw something back.
- Plant some thyme in your garden of life. Take thyme for fun, thyme for rest, and thyme for yourself.
- Stay in love! Did you know that being in a state of love releases positive energies to flow freely around your body and they cure any number of ailments?
- Do the things you can and let God handle the things you can't.

"The great thing about getting older is that you don't lose all the other ages you've been."

—*Madeline L' Engle*

Why is it that as people get older they have a tendency to relegate romance only to the young? I guess this comes from the false notion that as you grow older, passions cool. Personally, I say it's just the opposite. Aged love is like aged wine; it becomes more satisfying, more refreshing, more valuable, more appreciated, and more intoxicating. Love and romance are sacred and should be treasured and respected, and its true value should not be underestimated. Just as your body needs nutrition and exercise, your mind and romantic side requires all those yesterdays to build on. Forgive those people with an incomplete understanding of romance, and as for you, drink fully from and cherish those wonderful yesterdays. Life will become richer, more beautiful, and happier.

Thoughts to Ponder

- Isn't it wonderful to know the more you invest in a marriage, the more valuable it is?
- Life is what you make of it—Kinda like clay-dah.
- At any age people love that human touch—holding hands, a warm hug, or just a friendly pat on the back.
- Your grandkids are a great help in your golden years—they help you get there faster!

"You cannot live only for yourself. A thousand fibers connect you with your fellow man, and in the threads of those fibers is sympathy. So remember: your actions run as causes, and they come back as effects."
—*Herman Melville*

Early in life we were encouraged to develop a strong competitive spirit at home, in play, and at work. This competitive quest for success and your built-in desire for being the best often work to the detriment to that cooperative spirit that is necessary to bring triumph. The quest is "okay," but you must keep in mind the best way to win comes through cooperation, compromise, caring, and utilizing your inner resources. Adopt an attitude of "one for all and all for one" to generate good causes, and they will come back as good effects. When you become a master at this skill, you will have tapped into your potential for becoming the best person you can be, for enjoying life to the fullest, and, best of all, everybody wins. May all your causes have successful effects!

Thoughts to Ponder

- You can tell a lot about a person by the way he or she handles a rainy day, lost luggage, and tangled Christmas tree lights.
- Don't be afraid to encounter risks. It is by taking chances that you learn how to be brave.
- Your difficulties are not in vain because whatever you learn from them you will be able to pass along to others.
- They say golf is like life, but don't believe them. Golf is more complicated than that.

"You can make more friends in two months by becoming interested in other people than you can in two years of trying to get other people interested in you."
—*Dale Carnegie*

Without a doubt the easiest way to make friends is to be a friend who cares and shows compassion. Taking an interest in others, caring, and showing genuine concern can be most fulfilling. Taking interest and showing compassion is not necessarily saying the right thing at the right time, but to leave unsaid the wrong thing at any given time. For one human being to love and feel compassion for another can be very challenging, but when you take actions and respond with an open heart, you will usually make the right decision. Compassion reaches far beyond your own life, has positive effects on the life of others, and can transform the world in ways you could never imagine. In the end, the measure of your life will be the total of your compassion, love, and those selfless moments that you have shared.

Thoughts to Ponder

- Plant squash seeds in your personal friendship garden today—squash gossip, squash indifference, squash grumbling, and squash selfishness.
- As a good friend you should be radical—you should love them when they are unlovable, hug them when they are un-huggable, and bear them when they are unbearable.
- Did you know you are just about as happy as you make up your mind to be?
- Prove your friendship with your compassion, love, and a grateful heart, but keep the right attitude about it.

> *"The measure of man's humanity is the extent and intensity of his love for mankind."*
> —*Ashley Montagu*

Have you ever been introduced to someone and said to yourself, *I know this type?* Wouldn't it be wonderful if you could just accept everyone you meet as individuals with dignity and believe they are good and truly honest? People are worthy of your respect simply because they are human and are one of God's creations and, no matter the circumstances, should be viewed with a positive outlook. Loving your family and friends and being kind and accepting to others for who they are will always bring out the best in you. This may well be the measure of your humanity, and if you can do this, you will have learned the most important lesson that love and caring can teach you.

Thoughts to Ponder

- Let go of those super-high standards for yourself and others. You can be happy in an imperfect world.
- Doesn't "expecting the unexpected" make the unexpected expected?
- Never humiliate another person. Always give them an honorable way to back down or out of a sticky situation and still save face.
- Love is a do-it-yourself project. Although it's difficult to do, God promises to reveal our wisdom when we respect others and control our words.

"On this earth, though far and near, without love, there's only fear."

—*Pearl S. Buck*

We never know the love of our parents until we become parents ourselves. They love you now and forever with an affection and fondness, which no action, no misery, and no crime of yours can do away with. The good news is that just as your parents love you and your children love you, your Heavenly Father loves you. The following saying tells you a little about how much the Heavenly Father cares:

"If He had a refrigerator, your picture would be on it. If He had a wallet, your photo would be in it. He sends you flowers every spring, a sunrise every morning, and a sunset every evening. When you want to talk, He will listen, and He could live anywhere in the universe, yet He chooses your heart."

That Christmas gift He sent you in Bethlehem should tell you He's crazy about you! And knowing and sharing his love will take away your fear.

Thoughts to Ponder

- In your garden of love plant some bay leafs. Bay leaf in yourself; bay leaf in your loved ones, and most of all, bay leaf in the Supreme Being who can restore your bay leaf when all obstacles seem to go against you.
- Just one person saying to me, "You've made my day!" makes my day.
- Worry concentrates on yesterday or tomorrow, so why not commit today to God and leave the worrying to Him?
- I don't say my golf game is bad, but I fear that if I grew tomatoes they'd come up sliced.

"People want riches. They need fulfillment."
—*Bob Conklin*

The fulfillment of your dreams, your peace of mind, your happiness, and your emotional contentment are determined by you. Each of us is given our own space and our own piece of the planet, and since it isn't a fixed spot, you can't leave it behind or lose it. It just follows you around. Wherever you are, at any given time or place, is where your space resides. What you do with it is of your own choosing, and as such, you can decorate it with kindness and love, paint it a solemn black of negativism, invite others in, or shut them out. You can keep it small by doing nothing or expand it by pursuing your dreams. As such, your fulfillment can be met by setting the temperature, adjusting the weather, creating the atmosphere for yourself. No one can come in and disrupt the mood you create unless you allow them. For better or for worse, the choice is always yours.

Thoughts to Ponder

- When you were born, you were crying and everyone around you was smiling. Live your life so that when you die, you're smiling and everyone around you is crying.
- Have you ever experienced a child falling asleep in your arms? It is one of the most peaceful feelings you can have in this world.
- Surprise your spouse with flowers and a romantic dinner for no reason other than to express your appreciation and love.
- I don't exercise at all. If God meant me to touch my toes, he would have put them farther up my body.

"If you want a friendship message to be heard, it has got to be sent out. To keep your love lamp burning, you have to keep putting oil in it."

—*Mother Theresa*

Someone once said, "There is no use waiting for your love boat to come in unless you've sent it out." What I think of as true love, others think of or explain as a "kindred-spirit friendship." Kindred-spirit friendship means that your love as a friend should be radical, fanatical, and most of all, mathematical! That means you should multiply the joy, divide the sorrow, subtract the past, and add to tomorrow, calculate the need deep in your heart, and you should always be bigger than the sum of all those parts. When you put this type of effort into your love lamp, there will be no waiting for the boat to come in. So send out your kindred-spirit friendship messages now. Don't wait for a better day.

Thoughts to Ponder

- I've learned that words harshly spoken are as difficult to retrieve as feathers in a gale.
- May my golfing buddies' golf balls lie in green pastures, and not in still waters.
- Have you ever been told the most inflammable kind of wood is a chip on your shoulder?
- As long as there are tests, there will be prayer in public schools.

"There is more hunger for love and appreciation in this world than for bread."
—*Unknown*

Do you feel you are a loving caring person when saying, "I love my car," "I love my new coat," or "I love spaghetti and meatballs"? Isn't it strange how easy it is to express your appreciation of an inanimate object, yet you have grave difficulty in verbalizing your appreciation and care for other human beings, even to those closest to you? The message "I care for you and appreciate you" is not something that goes without saying. To the contrary, it needs to be said whenever and wherever! Sometimes all a person needs is a hand to hold and a heart to understand. Do your share to lessen the "worldwide" hunger for love by demonstrating your care and appreciation to those you love.

Thoughts to Ponder

- Any action that inhibits is not love. Love is only love when it liberates.
- Money is an article, which may be used as a universal passport to everywhere except heaven and as a universal provider of everything except happiness.
- Did you know Noah said, "No matter the storm, when your God is with you, there's a rainbow waiting"?
- I've learned that no matter how serious your life requires you to be, everyone needs a friend to act goofy with.

"When your problems seem to be unsolvable and all best efforts are frustrated, it is lifesaving to listen to and think of other people's problems."

—Unknown

Maybe you are better off than you think. Take a look around and listen to and think about the many problems of others compared to yours. You could be happier than you think but are so busy concentrating on the negative you can't see the positive side of life or, as the saying goes, "You can't see the forest for the trees." Regretting the things you did will be tempered by time but wasting time regretting the things you did not do is a surefire way to feel miserable. Remember pain and suffering are inevitable but misery is optional. Maybe it's time to be sick and tired of being sick and tired and make some attitude adjustments. When the situation appears to be unsolvable and your mind keeps concentrating on the big picture, it can be overwhelming. Take a step backward, you may need to dissect it and look at achieving small successes in order to move forward. Similar to working on that 1000-piece puzzle, you will succeed only when you think positive and think small. Total success is made up of the little things accomplished and eventually those small delights will constitute blissfulness. It's your choice! Either you try to enjoy the little things in life or you don't.

Thoughts to Ponder

- Being defeated is often a temporary condition because giving up is what makes it permanent.
- Have you ever thought that your depression is nothing more than your body saying it needs work?
- Be happy, don't let anything burst your balloon, boogie through life, and don't regret the things you didn't do.
- Did you ever stop to think and then forget to start again?

"The applause of a single human being is of great consequence."

—*Samuel Johnson*

Everyone is in need of being appreciated, to be the recipient of that most supreme compliment, and to know that we are loved or that we make a difference. We all need to recognize others' strengths and to recognize when they need to be propped up in the places where they tend to lean a little. A good friend is the one who tells you how you really look in your jeans. Honest compliments are simple and cost nothing to give, but we must not underestimate their worth. I read about a Mr. Choate, who, when asked who he would like to be if he could come back to earth again after he died, replied, "Mrs. Choate's second husband." Wow! Isn't that great?

Thoughts to Ponder

- Did you know every person you meet in life has a flashing sign on his or her chest? It says, "Make me feel special."
- Master your time and you win. Do what's important now.
- Though it may feel good at the time, talking negatively about someone will only bring hurt and destruction.
- Noah was told that for safety's sake they should travel in pairs, but why didn't Noah swat those *two* mosquitoes?

> *"The thoughtless are rarely wordless."*
> —*Howard W. Newton*

There is nothing more destructive and demeaning than the casual putdown. Yet on occasion we belittle each other with sarcastic comments in an attempt to change the other's behavior or attitude. When the narrow-minded, wide-mouth approach is used, many unforeseen problems can be created, and instead of the intended results of change expected, you usually get aggravation and retaliation. So if you think you have influence over someone, why resort to methods that wound and have the power to destroy when you can just as easily treat them kindly? When selecting your responses, remember, between two negative remarks choose neither, but between two positive ones always choose both. It's easy to say, "Treat others as you would like to be treated," but it is the follow through that will be worthwhile.

Thoughts to Ponder

- Envying others is a waste of time and, like an acid, it eats away at the container in which it is held.
- Don't use time or words carelessly because neither can be retrieved.
- Two things are hard on the heart—running up stairs and running down people.
- Blessed are those who have nothing to say and refrain from giving wordy evidence of that fact.

> *"The mind of the bigot is like the pupil of the eyes; the more light you pour upon it, the more it will contract."*
> —*Oliver Wendell Holmes Jr.*

When you classify or try to fit people into convenient categories, it tends to minimize their worth or exclude them from being accepted without thoughtful reason. Many of us will use a number of excuses to distance ourselves from those who are different than we are. Yet in reality, grouping people just saves us the trouble of thinking independently and evaluating each individual as a separate, distinct, and deserving person. It has been said that the scorpion carries his poison in his tail and the slanderer carries it in his tongue. Emerson, speaking of a simple weed, called it "a plant whose virtues have not yet been discovered." You may be surprised to find that they are not weeds, but rather flowers that you have failed to stop long enough to appreciate. When you meet those who are different from you, try not to label them, just as you would want them to not label you. Only you and your love can discard those labels and help on your journey of discovery.

Thoughts to Ponder

- If you don't stoop down, you will never be able to lift others up.
- The practice of honesty is more convincing than the profession of holiness.
- What you have done for yourself dies with you. What you have done for others and the world will remain immortal.
- I've learned that the greater a person's sense of guilt, the greater his or her need to cast blame on others.

"To live in the hearts we leave behind is not to die."
—*Thomas Cambell*

You never lose the people you love, even to death. They will continue to participate in every act, thought, and decision you make. Love leaves an indelible imprint in your memory, and you can take comfort in knowing that since you have shared love, it now enriches your life. Take heart in knowing that you are enriched for having loved and being loved, and your memories of that love transcend even death. Knowing that you have shared your love is to know that you will live on in the hearts of others and your life does make a difference. Live in contentment today and move forward by reflecting on the memories of the good times of your shared love.

Thoughts to Ponder

- Faith does not demand miracles, but often accomplishes them.
- A sad thing about life is sometimes you meet a person who means a lot to you only to find out in the end that it was never meant to be and you just have to let go.
- Under everyone's hard shell is someone who wants to be appreciated and loved. (Try it, you'll like it!)
- Statistics show that at the age of seventy, there are five women to every man. Isn't that the darndest time for a guy to get those odds?

"Love and caring and trust are fruits in season at all times and within the reach of every hand."
—*Unknown*

Sometimes the purest demonstrations of love and care surface through casual, spontaneous encounters, such as someone stopping to help you with a flat tire, showing genuine concern, offering to help in times of need, or just giving you a hug. It is important to take the time to positively acknowledge when another person momentarily enriches your life with a touch of care or love. "Love, caring, and trust enhance love and caring and trust." So bring that love and trust into your life by focusing each day on those who care about you and on those you care most about in this world, whom you most respect and admire, and give all your attention and time to them.

Thoughts to Ponder

- No matter what their ages or how far away they may be, you never stop wanting to keep a protective arm around your children.
- If you're feeling confused, don't even begin to think it's from God. He brings peace, not turmoil.
- An old Chinese Proverb says, "When someone shares something of value with you and you benefit from it, you have a moral obligation to share it with others."
- Make sure everything in your house is useful, beautiful, or delicious.

"Some people feel with their heads and think with their hearts."
—G. C. Lichtenberg

Have you ever attempted to influence or change the ways of another human being by threatening to withhold your caring or your love? You certainly have heard, known, or used a statement like, "I will love you if..." "I will love you if you stay home," "I will love you if you are successful," or "I will love you if you agree with me." In many cases these negative-type messages are hurtful and have the opposite results of those intended. Instead of a negative message, send a positive one, such as, "I will care for and love you, even if your hair falls out," or "Don't worry about losing my love. You're stuck with me 'til the end of time." Remember, no human creature can give orders for someone to change their personality or to love another. When sending positive messages, you are like a candle that loses nothing by lighting another candle.

Thoughts to Ponder

- If you are lucky enough to find someone who genuinely cares about you, never let him or her go.
- The kind of adults your children become is directly related to the kind of children that you told them they were.
- Positive influences can be addictive.
- Giving and truly loving other people changes the kind of person you are.

> *"Those who do not know to weep with their whole heart don't know how to laugh either."*
> —*Golda Meir*

Science recently proved that tears of emotion contain one of the brain chemicals known to be painkillers. When you are in the midst of the trials of troubled times, such as death or a broken heart, there is little comfort in being told, "This will pass," "Keep a stiff upper lip," or "Love will eventually intervene and heal you." Pain may crack the heart, but tears offer you a chance to heal and laugh again. Remember, there is nothing quite so satisfying—or healing—as a good cry, especially since you now know it's a big step in healing.

Thoughts to Ponder

- As you grow up, you have your heart broken probably more than once, and it's harder every time.
- One sincere apology is worth more than all the roses money can buy.
- If it's true that we are here to help others, then what exactly are the others here for?
- The one thing that unites all human beings, regardless of age, gender, religion, economic status, or ethnic background, is the fact that, deep down inside, we all believe we are above-average drivers, and everyone else who drives is a maniac.

"He who wants to do good knocks at the gate. He who loves finds the gate open."
—*Rabindranath Tagore*

When you want to do good, sometimes you need to change your strategy. If you always do what you've always done, you will always get what you've always gotten. Here is a little hint in using your gift of love: don't just be a knocker; become a lover. Start by being more charitable, giving people a break, blessing instead of condemning, supporting instead of deriding, forgiving instead of attacking, and projecting all that love you have been hiding instead of indifference and shyness. Your true love should always be bestowed as a gift—freely, willingly, and without expectation. It should be offered even when not acknowledged or appreciated, and remember, sometimes it's not *what* you say, it's *how* you say it. It's wonderful to know that you don't love to be loved; you should love to love, and when you are in love it shows.

Thoughts to Ponder

- The world would be a better place if you would visit an elderly neighbor or a convalescent home.
- The world is your looking glass and gives back to you the reflection of your own face.
- Ignoring the facts does not change the facts.
- God loves you. Matthew 7:7–8 says, "Ask and it shall be given to you, seek and you will find, knock and the door shall be opened to you."

"We are emotional beings, and emotion has taught mankind to reason."

—*Marquis De Vauvenargues*

When expressing your feelings, do you often find yourself being unreasonable, illogical, and self-centered? Your emotions usually dictate your actions, and how you express your feelings to others says much about your mental health and how they accept you. Knowing this fact, you may want to choose to be delicate, diplomatic, and to hold your emotions in check. You may choose to let them fly free with a "no-holds-barred philosophy," but in most cases that's the wrong choice. Examine your actions, and remember that you generally survive your expressed feelings, but you have to live with the consequences of those expressed emotions and actions. Common sense and sensitivity should be your best guides, and if you ultimately feel better about yourself, others will feel better about themselves.

Thoughts to Ponder

- Guess what? The person who talks about his inferiors hasn't any.
- If you are kind to others, people may accuse you of selfish ulterior motives. Be kind anyway.
- Feel better today; toot your own horn, pull out all the stops, add fuel to the fire, and hit the nail on the head.
- The Lord is never up in heaven wringing His hands, upset about what has happened on earth. He has always known and always has a plan.

"It is with the heart that one can see rightly. What is essential is invisible to the eye."
—*Antoine De Saint—Exupery*

Where there is no faith, there can be no love. Love is not love unless it is transferred or expressed. When your newly born child or grandchild holds on to your little finger with his or her tiny hand, in your heart you're hooked for life. It's invisible, but in that moment of serenity and happiness the transfer of love strengthens your faith in love. As a human being, a spouse, or a parent, what else do we have to give that costs us so little? What else is so inexhaustible in supply as your love? What else confers benefits to both the giver and the receiver with so little effort? I pray that you have lots and lots of faith, and remember this: Pascal once said, "Faith is different from proof: the latter is human, the former is from God."

Thoughts to Ponder

- Love is like a rock thrown into a pond, causing the ripples to gradually keep going out across the entire lake. Our acts of love influence the entire human race in the same way.
- The good you do today may often be forgotten tomorrow, but you should do good anyway.
- It's your memories, not money, that make you rich!
- When someone loves you, the way they say your name is different. You just know that your name is safe in their mouth.

> *"Love is patient, love is kind, it does not envy, it does not boast, it is not rude, it is not self-seeking; it is not easily angered. It keeps no record of wrong; it does not delight in evil, but rejoices with the truth. It always protects, always trusts, always hopes, and always perseveres."*
> —*1 Corinthians* 13:4–7

"True love" is a mixture of human love and spiritual love. The above quote from 1 Corinthians expresses the ultimate goal of true love. Although faith-based, it is spiritually inspired, and its human application creates an open feeling and affiliation with all of life, or what we call "unconditional love." Human love involves your personal needs and is based on your physical and emotional needs, as well as your mental state. Human love, in many cases, is not necessarily spiritual or unconditional. When you have faith and understand the differences, your heart will allow you to enter into that special realm and you can then give your love unconditionally. If the truth were known, it would be that you could only enter an unconditional love realm when your physical, emotional, mental, and spiritual needs have been met.

Thoughts to Ponder

- Loving others takes understanding, which is easy when you use the Bible as a "how-to book."
- If you ever find love by hunting for it, you will find it as the old woman did her lost spectacles—safe on her nose.
- The doors to love are marked with "Push" and "Pull."
- Love is what makes you smile when you're tired.

"There are no problems, only solutions."
—*John Lennon*

You cannot pick or choose your problems, they just happen upon us. But with a little thought you can choose what to do about them. Someone once said, "You cannot solve life's problems except by solving them." Step back from your problems, provide time to analyze, reorganize, and begin to realize the solution. The right attitude and distancing yourself from a seemingly hopeless situation can help you engage in the steps to solve the situation. For some the solution is just positive thinking—not complaining because of rainy weather, but being thankful that the grass is getting watered for free; not grumbling about aches and pains but rejoicing about being alive. For others the sources may require counselors, friends, family, books, and work associates. When you are confronted with problems, you can either choose to be a victim or you can seek solutions. When you choose to solve them, be certain that you learn from them!

Thoughts to Ponder

- If someone says something unkind about you, you should react and live in a way so that no one will believe it.
- Now that you know money is not everything and you can't have too much, please send the extra to me *immediately*.
- In school did they teach you that if you tell the truth, you don't have to remember anything?
- You may think anger motivates, but it doesn't. Only encouragement can. Gentle words bring great benefits.

> *"Anyone who keeps the ability to see beauty is never old."*
> —*Franz Kafka*

When you are down and out and things seem grim, the last thing you want to do is to resort to a world of worthless self-pity. Avoid this emotion like the plague and rise above it by giving yourself a "shot in the arm" of encouragement. The shot should include your greatest asset (your faith), your best attire (your smile), and your most contagious spirit (your enthusiasm). Use the most incredible computer in the world, which is your brain, to concentrate and focus on the beauty that surrounds you today. Experience more of life by using the limitless scope of your mind and all of its senses to increase your ability to appreciate beauty. Watch a sunset with someone, observe the birds flying overhead, listen to music, or enjoy a beautiful painting. No matter the weather, take a walk in the park with someone you care for. The beauty and worthiness of the Lord's creation never grows old if you take the time to sit back and enjoy.

Thoughts to Ponder

- The best and most beautiful things in the world cannot be seen or touched, but are felt in the heart.
- A rich person is not the one who has the most, but is the one who needs the least.
- Life is your greatest possession and love is your greatest declaration.
- When a child is nurtured by loving parents, heaven doesn't seem like such a faraway place.

> *"The greatest discovery of my generation is that human beings alter their lives by altering their attitudes of mind."*
>
> —*William James*

Isn't it wonderful that in our time men and women can now discover their real selves? Men cry, cook, enjoy theater and ballet, raise children, and openly express their love. Women can be major providers, lift weights, box, play football, and openly express their love. It's wonderful how members of each gender can express their uniqueness as human beings while becoming successful. Our generation has been willing to risk all they have gained for the things they believe in and trust. Simply by altering their attitudes they have not only altered their own lives, but have changed the attitude of the world as it was once known. And when they work together for common goals, the benefits to humanity are astronomical.

Thoughts to Ponder

- Balance your life between time spent alone and time spent with others.
- Never give up a good chance to shut up!
- Fires burn out when left unattended. Work together and rekindle your personal relationship fire on a daily basis.
- You are on the road to success when you realize that failure is merely a detour.

> *"We do have choice, but not without some agony."*
> —*Josephine Hart*

When you have problems at home or at work, you often feel a change can help resolve your problems. You may be thinking of a new job, a new location, a new apartment, a new house, or maybe a new companion. The only problem with these choices is that you have to take "you" along wherever you go. If you are down and out in Texas, chances are you will be down and out in California, New York, or Washington. In today's society it is too easy to move on down the road with very little motivation to stay with and work at relationships. Changing partners in the middle of a dance is at the very best a temporary fix. When in doubt, here are a few thoughts to remember: never say goodbye when you still want to try; never give up when you feel you still care; and never say you don't love that person if you can't let go. Changes have to be made from within instead of without. There is no other way.

Thoughts to Ponder

- Wasting your money only means you're out of money, but when you waste your time, you lose a part of your life.
- People who make a difference in your life are not the ones with the most credentials, the most money, or the most awards. They are the ones who care.
- When you lose, don't forget the lesson.
- You can lose a workday in many ways. But can you tell me one way to get that day back?

"Most of us are taught from an early age to pay far more attention to the signals coming from other people than from those within. We are encouraged to ignore our own needs and wants and to concentrate on living up to other's expectations."

—*Unknown*

You have a basic right as a human being to be accepted as yourself. Disapproval by others is not enough reason or an excuse to strive to be less than who you truly are. Sometimes it seems as if those around us remake us into something we really don't want to be. Whether it is through indifference, weakness, or ignorance, you give up control of yourself to others. Allowing yourself to be dominated or controlled by them relinquishes your individuality. It may now be the time to concentrate on you and become what you believe you should be. Your success and happiness are based largely on your sense of self-worth and having a clear picture of who you really are. So if you want to be treated as who you really are, you must live up to your own expectations. Someone once said, "Man is what he believes he is." Are you?

Thoughts to Ponder

- Did you know that if you are still talking about what you did yesterday, you haven't done much today?

- Anything you do that may blemish your integrity is more than wrong; it is shameful!

- By living your life one day at a time, you live *all* the days of your life. So don't let life slip through your fingers by living in the past or for the future.

- If you think nobody cares whether you're alive, try missing a couple of car payments.

> *"Difficult times have helped us to understand how infinitely rich and beautiful life is. Yet we sometimes worry about so many things that are of no importance whatsoever."*
>
> —*Isak Dinesen*

After you survive a difficult and trying situation in your life, it pays to take the time to and analyze the overall positive pieces of your life. I have found it's much easier to remember the happy experiences and the high-quality times rather than the unpleasant. It's natural to not reflect on the experiences of poor decisions unless you learned some valuable lessons from those poor decisions. It is also a waste of time. Surviving and moving on is why you are where you are today! When you are grateful for the blessings you have been given, you give yourself the possibility to understand the richness and beauty of life itself. Remember, life is in every sunset, every flower's unfolding petal, every baby's smile, every lover's kiss, and every wonderful, astonishing, miraculous beat of your heart. God gave up something very special for you, and if you have faith it will make your up-look good, your outlook bright, and your in-look favorable. Best of all, it will enrich your future.

Thoughts to Ponder

- You begin to appreciate what's important when you can find the best in others.
- Each day take a positive action. Your life depends on it!
- Learn to greet everyone with a smile. They deserve it!
- Learn to gather all the crumbs thrown your way and they soon will form a lovely thick slice of life and memories.

"It is man's destiny to ponder on the riddle of existence, of his wonderment, and how to create a new life on this earth."

—Charles F. Kettering

For some of us it is difficult to remember being children, but for others it is very easy to remember that time of "not too long ago." As adults we remember that as children our faith was unwavering, our joy was a natural state, we had no worry, and there was plenty of laughing and playing. In reality not much has changed other than our attitude and the way we choose to look at things. The future can still have the wonder, excitement, mystery, magic, and fun it once had if you just look for them. The next time you wish that you could return to the good old days, remember that anything is possible, but don't look or wait for it to happen. Use your rearview mirror as a guidance tool. Enjoy the ride of existence and the wonderment, but keep your eye on the road ahead.

Thoughts to Ponder

- Start a "victory" journal and write down every success you have.
- Don't let a bad day affect how you treat your family.
- The Lord's definition of prosperity is different for each of us. He wants you to succeed in the special plan He has developed for you.
- Something to ponder would be why lemon juice is made with artificial flavor and dish soap is made with real lemons.

"At the banquet of life, soul is our appetite. People filled with the hunger of the soul take food from every dish, whether it be sweet or bitter."
—*Matthew Fox, Ph. D.*

It has been said that "God delights in watching the soul grow." If true it would be a good idea to seek some soul nourishment and to begin feasting on life's banquet today. Whether each day's soul feeding from the banquet is a feast or famine depends upon your attitude. With a positive attitude, creating, enjoying humor, failure, righting a wrong, facing a sorrow head on, meditation, disappointment, and, yes, even work will contribute to easing the hunger. Nourishment begins by knowing what you want and setting your heart and mind to believing you can get it. Most important is the knowledge of knowing that you do not necessarily require happiness at all times. As the quote says, "Whether bitter or sweet, take from every dish."

Thoughts to Ponder

- If you have weeds growing in your garden, you need to take time to work on what you planted.
- For those who love God, laughter isn't optional; it is scriptural.
- Being at the dinner table with your family and cherished friends, you will find the food better, the environment quieter, the cost much cheaper, and the pleasure much more fulfilling than anything else you might ordinarily do.
- I've learned the best things in life are falling in love, laughing so hard your face hurts, finding no lines at Kmart, a special glance, and getting mail from a friend.

"Let him that desires to see others happy convey his love and make haste while the gift can be enjoyed. Remember that every moment of delay takes away something from its value."

—*Samuel Johnson*

To enjoy life you have to share love. When you are in love, you experience your most profound feelings of joy, peace, security, and the wondrous feeling of togetherness. Feelings can fade away, and in some cases the one we love may seem distant and no longer the person they once were. Openness builds a foundation of rock on which to build your love, but don't make today's judgments on yesterday's memories. In real estate, the agents say, "Location, location, location." In loving relationships, partners say, "Communication, communication, communication." To withhold for even a day will diminish your relationship and take away from the value of it. To postpone it is a great human tragedy.

Thoughts to Ponder

- Don't delay; you never know what tomorrow will bring, and it may be too late.
- Isn't it nice to know forgiveness begins when the blame ends?
- One forgives to the degree one loves.
- Happiness is what happens to you; joy is something you choose. With happiness and joy in your life, it becomes infectious and sadness can't stay around.

"A man must see before he can say."
—*Henry David Thoreau*

When you're looking at life through rose-colored glasses, there are times when you see what you want to see rather than what really is. Whether your experiences are good, bad, beautiful, or ugly, there are going to be times you may not understand them. But if you can visualize them and act on them in a positive way, your life will take on a new zest with a deeper interest, and the experiences will have greater meaning for you. This is not looking through the rose-colored glasses, but rather accepting them, understanding them, and giving you the insight to tell others. You can now think excitement, talk out excitement, become excited, and tell others about the results of your positive thinking. You can be boastful now, knowing you can build up inspiration, excitement, and hope for others with the results of your actions.

Thoughts to Ponder

- If you are honest and frank, people may cheat you, but you should be honest and frank anyway!
- The fastest way to accomplish something is not by working as fast as you can, but as steadily as you can.
- Did you know that the easiest way for you to grow as a person is to surround yourself with people smarter than yourself?
- When things reach their absolute worst, remember this: "If you're going through hell, keep going."

"Feeling that I have assisted someone in a very positive manner in some little way or made their day a little brighter makes my writing of the celubrious messages a joy and a pleasure.

—*Dennis A. Martin*

Readers of my celubrious messages often ask why I continue to write them. Well, to tell the truth, by writing them each day my attitude remains positive, I walk around with a smile on my face, and one more page for this book is finished. However, the prime incentive is the feedback I get. When people express their appreciation and tell me that a certain message really hit home in their personal lives or made a difference in their day, helped them to see something in another way, or that they forwarded it to family members and friends, my motivation goes off the charts. One of my most cherished returns said, "Good sermon and reflection material" from Pastor Joe in Newton, Texas. How could it get any better than that? I love writing these messages, and my days are brighter and my daily work easier when I receive a compliment. Encourage someone today, tell someone you love them, thank them for being in your life, and express your honest feelings to your friends. Their day will be brighter and so will yours.

Thoughts to Ponder

- I've heard that it is wrong to suppress laughter. It goes back down and spreads to your hips.
- True friendship will continue to grow even over the longest distance, and the same goes for love.
- Uncanny, isn't it, that you can do something in an instant that will cause happiness or heartache for life?
- *May the Lord continue to hold you in the palm of His hand.*

Celubrious Message Endorsements

"Everyone should keep Celubrious and the Bible close at hand. When life seems dull, boring, or even depressing; when the rigors of work, school, or life in general get you down, pick up both and read a few pages of each. You will be a different person and have a fresh perspective on life."

-Rev. Dr. Joe Miller Jr.
Newton, Texas

I sincerely believe it was His will to have you sit next to me on the plane so that you could send me all the wonderful e-mails you send me. In that respect you have truly been a Godsend to me. What a wonderful God we have. And, as shown in this e-mail, what a beautiful world He has created! You have been an inspiration to me. Thank you so much for giving of yourself and your time.

-Cinthey

Thanks. God brought something into my life through you. Being reacquainted with my spiritual side has been the best thing that has happened to me for a long time. Today I asked God what I could do for Him, not the other way around. I am finally coming back around the circle. It has been a hard, hard struggle for me because I had lost my faith and did not know how to get it back. It is coming back. All I can do is say thanks.

-Jeanette

I just wanted to let you know how much I have enjoyed reading your morning inspirational messages. They seem to get me going in the right direction. What's really great is how they have changed me. To be honest I used to not even read them. I used to think I don't have time to read all those messages. But once I sincerely read my first one, I know I must make the time. Because time is what it is all about and how you spend it. Thanks for taking your time to send these great thoughts. "You've made my day!" everyday.

-Serene

Good one for me today as this is the first day of my new life as a minister.

-Thanks, Pastor Joe

Thank you for taking the time to motivate us on a daily basis. I have truly enjoyed the words of wisdom you send. Let us hope our positive attitudes will help bring about a more positive atmosphere here at work.

-Maralee

I love to read the daily message because it gets me outside of myself and I realize that I am not alone, I face the same things other people face, and I can make it because others before have and others after will. At times your daily message may be the only bright spot in a day coming from outside of me, though I will always have Christ within to sustain me. I wish more people shared the joy like you do, and I do pass these along to my friends. I hope they publish not just one but several books for you.

-Cindy

I really appreciate the good words. Jesus said, "I am the way the truth and the life." I forward your messages to my friends and my wife and they really appreciate them. Thanks and God bless you,

-Jimbo

Please keep me on your message list. While you were out earlier this week my day just did not start the same without your morning inspirational message. Some mornings I don't take the time to pray the way I should and in my own guilty way your message makes up for my negligence. Thanks and keep on inspiring all of us.

-Brenda

Messages like this are great tools to keep things in perspective. Thanks,

-Manfred

I *love* your good morning messages. Please keep 'em coming. Forever your friend!

-Jackie

I was not in a great mood when I read your message today. I told myself, "Right, life is wonderful when you have someone special. But when you don't have that someone special, then this message was sure a downer." Then I realized that I was the only one responsible if I allowed myself to become depressed because "no one loved me." How do I know that no one loves me? How do I know that maybe there may be someone out there who really loves me and I am looking at it the wrong way. As long as I know that God loves me that special way, then I don't need to see with my eyes a physical person who loves me. I have the best love that a person can have.

-Jeanette

Just last night I was pondering several "troubles" going on in our family right now, and I did make myself stop and just thank God for my many blessings, which *far* outweighed the troubling things. Your thoughts and tips are really absorbed each day. I look forward to them. I hope other coworkers enjoy these as much as I do.

-Theresa

Thank you for the morning message! It has pertained to me more than once and has helped me look at things in a positive way, instead of pessimistically. It has brought me out of a funk and uplifted me when hubby, money, or work gets me down. Anyway, thanks again.

-Suszan

Thank you. I passed it on to my family. This is so timely because we just got the word yesterday than one of my nephews just got diagnosed with liver cancer. He is only in his thirties.

PS—I am really enjoying your daily messages. It must take you some time to put these together. Have you considered publishing these?

-Pam

I have written you before and asked you if you had ever thought about doing a book. I think it would be wonderful, and I would buy it in a minute. With a book, I could throw away all your messages that I keep in a notebook at home. As for my favorites, I'm sure I have some, but they are at home and it would be very hard to choose. I send these on to two people and hope they will write you also.

-Sandra

Thank you so much for continuing your daily inspirational message. They have been a source of comfort and joy for me and my family. Somehow, your message seems to always suit our needs for something that is going on in our hectic lives. It gives us a chance to stop and reflect for a moment and catch our breath. I would also like to mention that I have been sharing your messages with several of my friends who also find them to be of great comfort. Please keep them coming as we all look forward to reading them to start our day. I am so happy that we had the opportunity to meet you and get to know you. Friends are a special gift sent from God who somehow knows just when to send that special gift into that person's life. Thanks again, Dennis ,and please stay in touch.

-Sandy

The morning messages assist all of us in life's true meaning. Keep up the work.

-Diana

I just wanted to let you know that I look forward to your mails. I am glad I am on your list because they really give me and the people I pass them on to a lift. Praying for you.

-Cindy

Thanks again for your daily words of inspiration. They have often been a source of motivation for me.

-Madison

Dennis, you certainly are at the top of your game today with your words of inspiration. Thank you very much.

I do forward to my niece in California and my nephew in Wyoming and my cousin in Maryland.

I forward your article each day to myself at home, where I then pass it to my daughters and son-in-law. Sometimes, I forward applicable things at random to other friends and/or relatives. Thanks for giving us good Thoughts to Ponder!

-Barbara

I pass these along to two people: one's an atheist and the other needs all the inspiration she can get! Thank you,

-Lisa

I am forwarding on your messages to four regulars who were interested in receiving them in Florida, Minnesota, and California. Keep up the good work.

-Mary Kay

I send your messages to approximately fifteen people depending on the content and who I think it might help by lifting spirits or by humor or just because. Sometimes I print them out and post them in my cubicle or pass them around by hardcopy. I also on occasion share them with people at church, which can vary from one to ten additional people.

I absolutely loved your tips about men. They were great! I can truly say I so look forward to getting your letter daily. They really make my day and also the day of the people I forward them on to.

-Diana

"A *Celubrious* quotation, thought, or reflection can help make your day, clarify your thinking, and give you unique inspiration. Inside this book is the perfect message for any situation, person, or attitude. To discover it when you need it most can be invaluable."

-Joann Detwiler
Canfield Christian Church Secretary

"These messages have become a source of inspiration, illumination, and insight to me. I have been personally blessed from these messages as they help set an inspirational tone and at times a challenge for my day. On occasion I have used *Celubrious Messages* as part of my sermons on Sunday at Canfield Christian Church. As a chaplain with Hospice of the Valley, I have used the *Celubrious Messages* to bring inspiration and comfort to those in sorrow and grief. At the end of life, families are broken and sorrowful over the loss of a loved one and I have used the content of the messages at funerals where appropriate. During some of our interdisciplinary team meetings covering our Hospice program deaths, I have shared message content and how I have applied some of the thoughts. The staff have found them encouraging and enlightening."

-Dr. John J. Eastman
Chaplain Hospice of the Valley
Minister, Canfield Christian Church
Canfield, Ohio

"This book has been a source of joy and encouragement that I have shared with my employers, coworkers, friends, and family. It has inspired them and countless others! This book is sure to motivate you, build your faith, and give you a positive attitude, no matter what life throws your way. Get ready to be blessed and have a "celubrious" day!

-Lisa M. Whitacre
Nashville, Tennessee

"I find myself picking up *Celubrious* on a regular basis. The messages are uplifting and encouraging. They have proven to be an inspiration to me and to others as I share the messages with family and friends. Many times I refer back to special messages that have helped me get through rough days. It's a great pick-me-up when I need it the most."

-Valerie Jernigan
Quality Coordinator
General Electric Company

"I have shared your thoughts with many people that I know because of the tremendous content. Your book is uplifting and motivational. The book has a tendency to bring out past experiences and instructions that we have received during our travel through life. It is purely a work of love and dynamic motivation! Everyone should be permitted to experience your wisdom and fruitful writings. Fruit for the soul!"

-Ray H. Wilkerson, MBA, Chief Master Sergeant, USAF (Retired), Lockheed Martin Aerospace Manager (Retired), Hi-Tech Engineering President
Corona, California

"The content of *Celubrious* has been a wonderful daily beginning to my personal days, right along with my first cup of coffee.

Besides my own 'jumpstart,' I have consistently shared these positive messages with many friends from coast to coast. So many times I hear back from the recipients that 'this is just what I needed today.'"

-Mary Kay Masquelier
McKinney, Texas

"I have many books on daily devotions, but by far I have found yours to be the most inspirational. The daily messages are brief yet pack a powerful message. I also refer back to some of the messages to help me get through trauma I have had in the past. Those messages from your book have hit right on what I am going through at the time and have helped me let go of much of the pain and move forward. I have also copied messages from your book and sent them to friends and they have responded back to me with such emotion."

-Linda Sorensen
Tampa, Florida

"This book is like a spiritual cup of coffee. Celubrious kickstarts my day and Dennis' timing is always right on with what is going on in my life. His inspiring words and thoughts to ponder seem to be just what I need to hear, and they always turn my attitude into gratitude."

-Sandi Banks
Fontana, California

Visit the Celubrious Web Site at www.celubrious.net .org and .com for daily motivation and inspiration. You can chat with and provide input for new pages and the development of upcoming books via the Web Site or by blogging at Mrcelubrious.blogspot.com or Celubrious@yahoogroups.com The author also tweets and is on Facebook. If inputs are used for future books; credit will be acknowledged with name and location if desired. Hard and Paperback books can be ordered from Tate Publishing at www.tatepublishing.com or personally signed copies can be ordered directly from Dennis at the Celubrious Web site. E-books are also available for Kindle and Tablets. All books can be ordered from you local book stores.